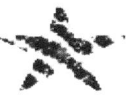

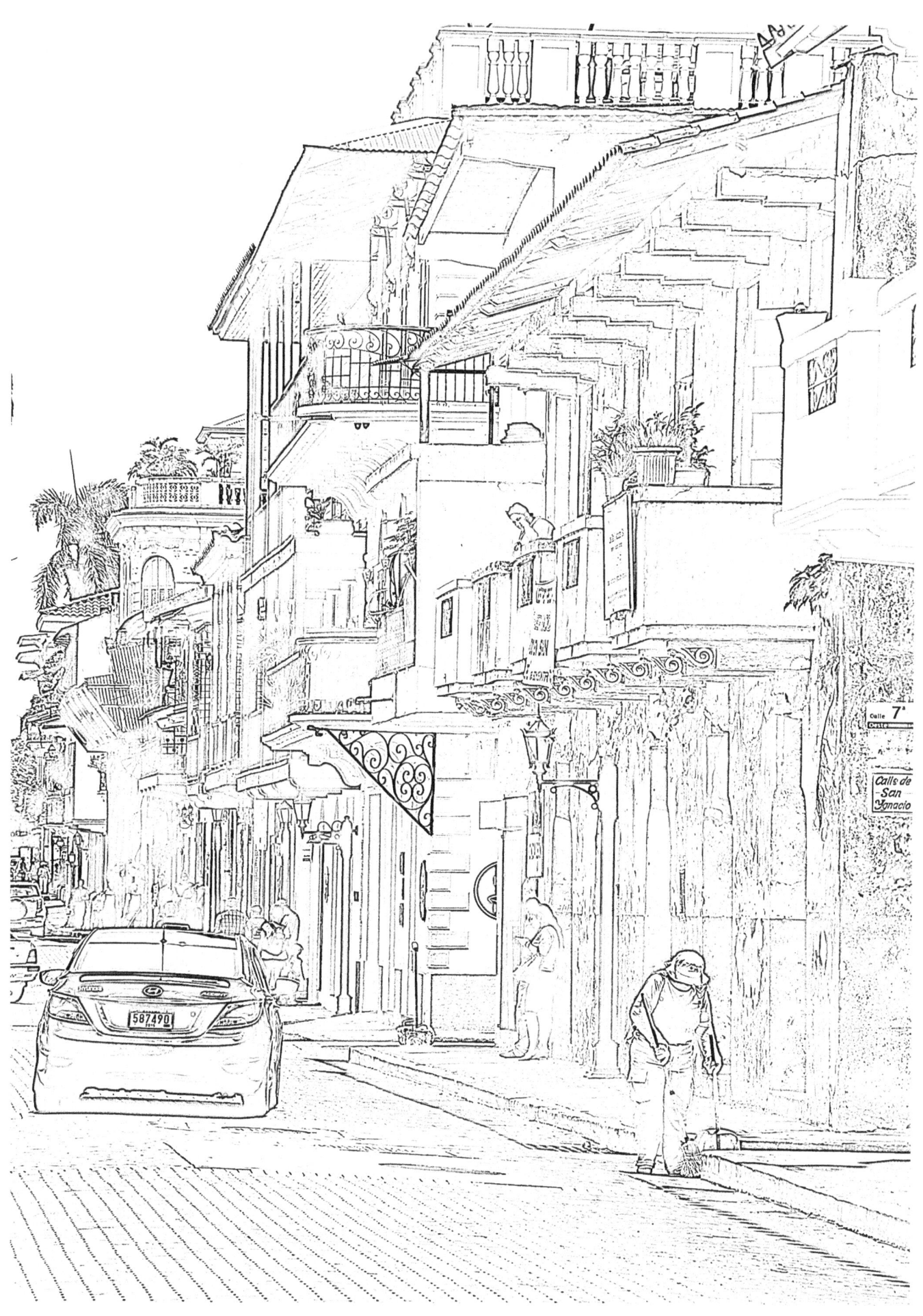

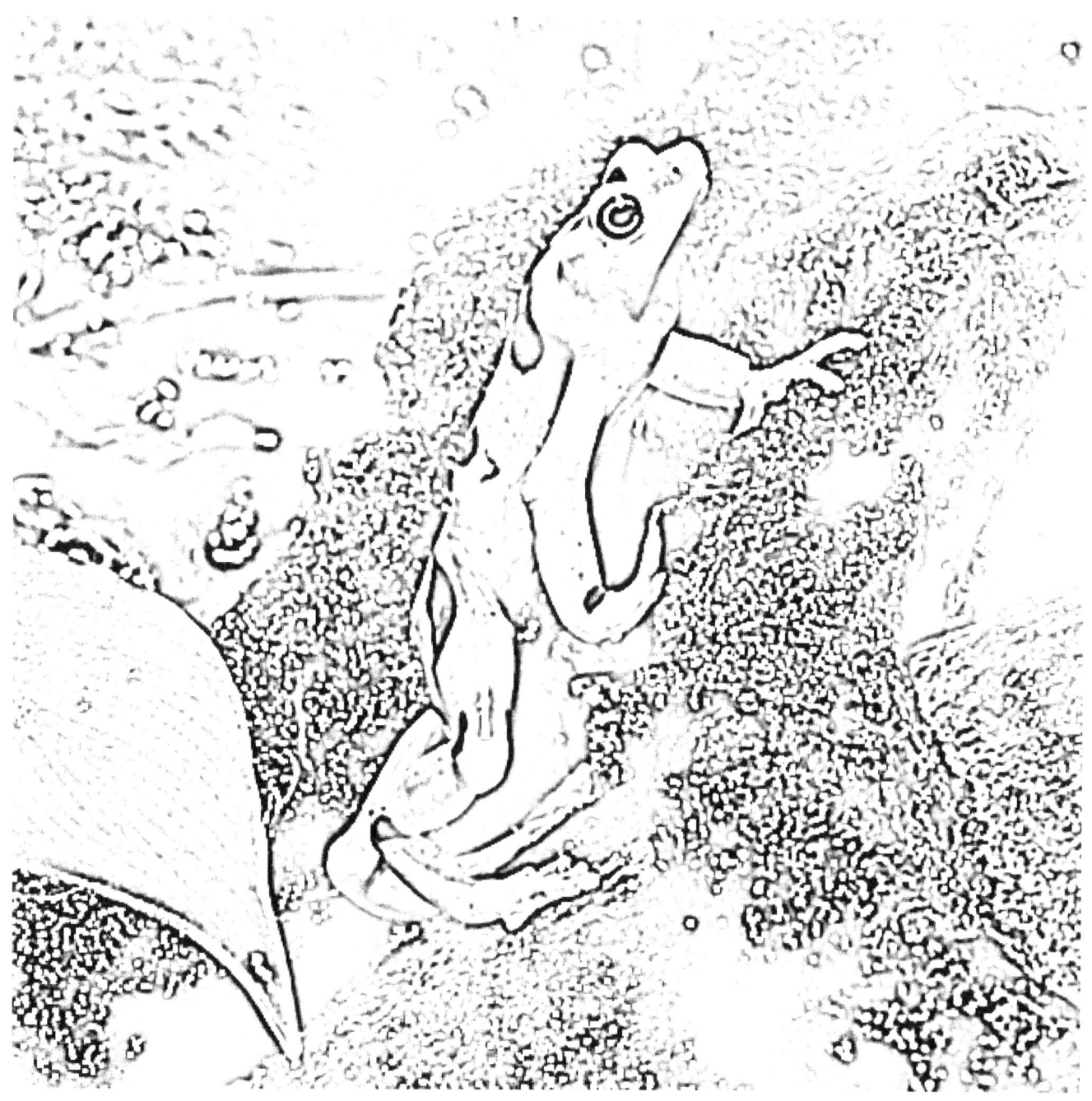

"GOLDEN FROG", "CASCO VIEJO", "PANAMA CANAL", "SLOTH", CANON BALL FLOWER", "HIBISCUS", "KUNA LADY", "POLLERA", "DIABLITOS", "PEDASI DESFILE DE CARRETAS", "RASPADO", "TUCAN" (Matt Tomlet)

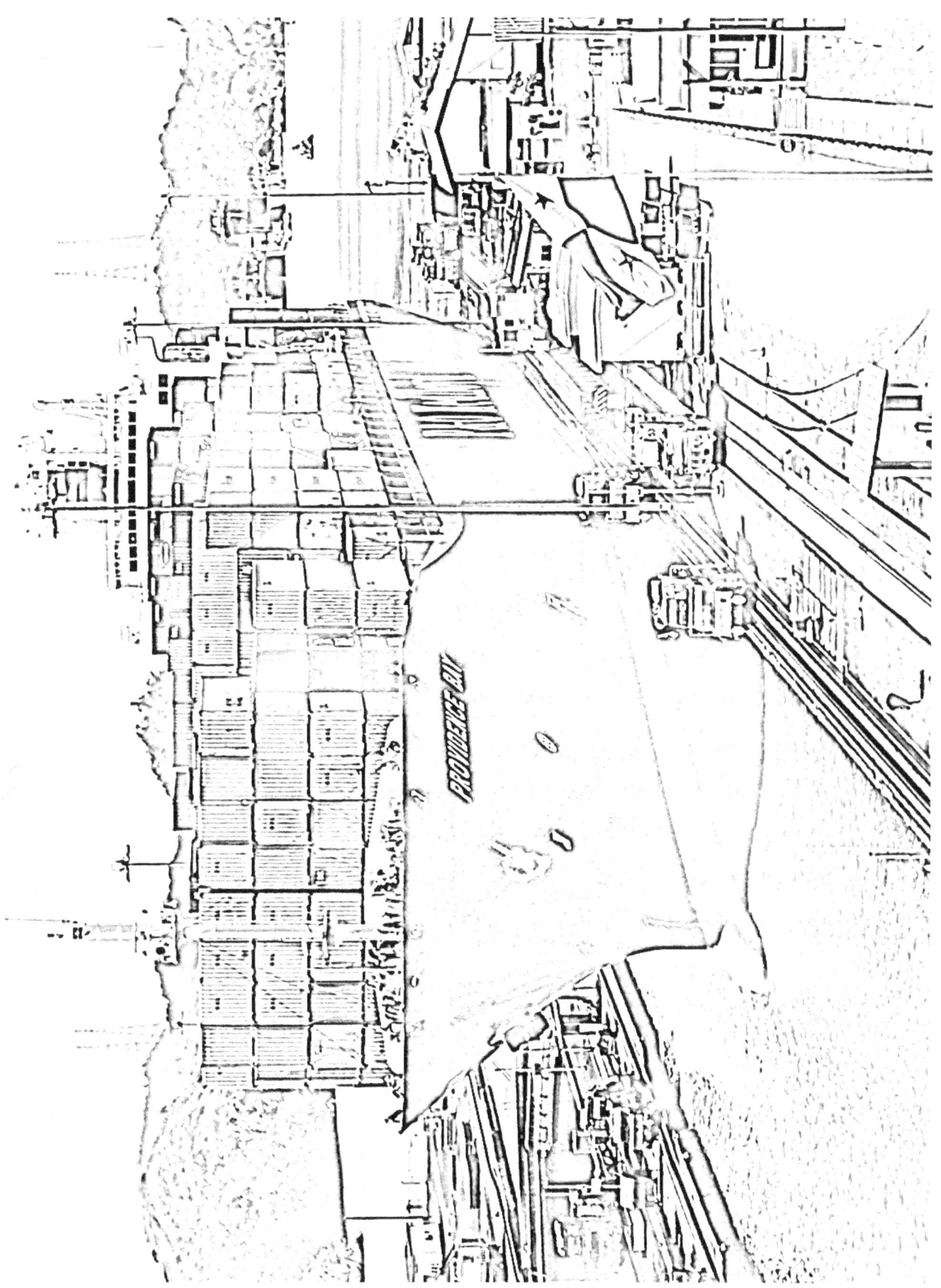

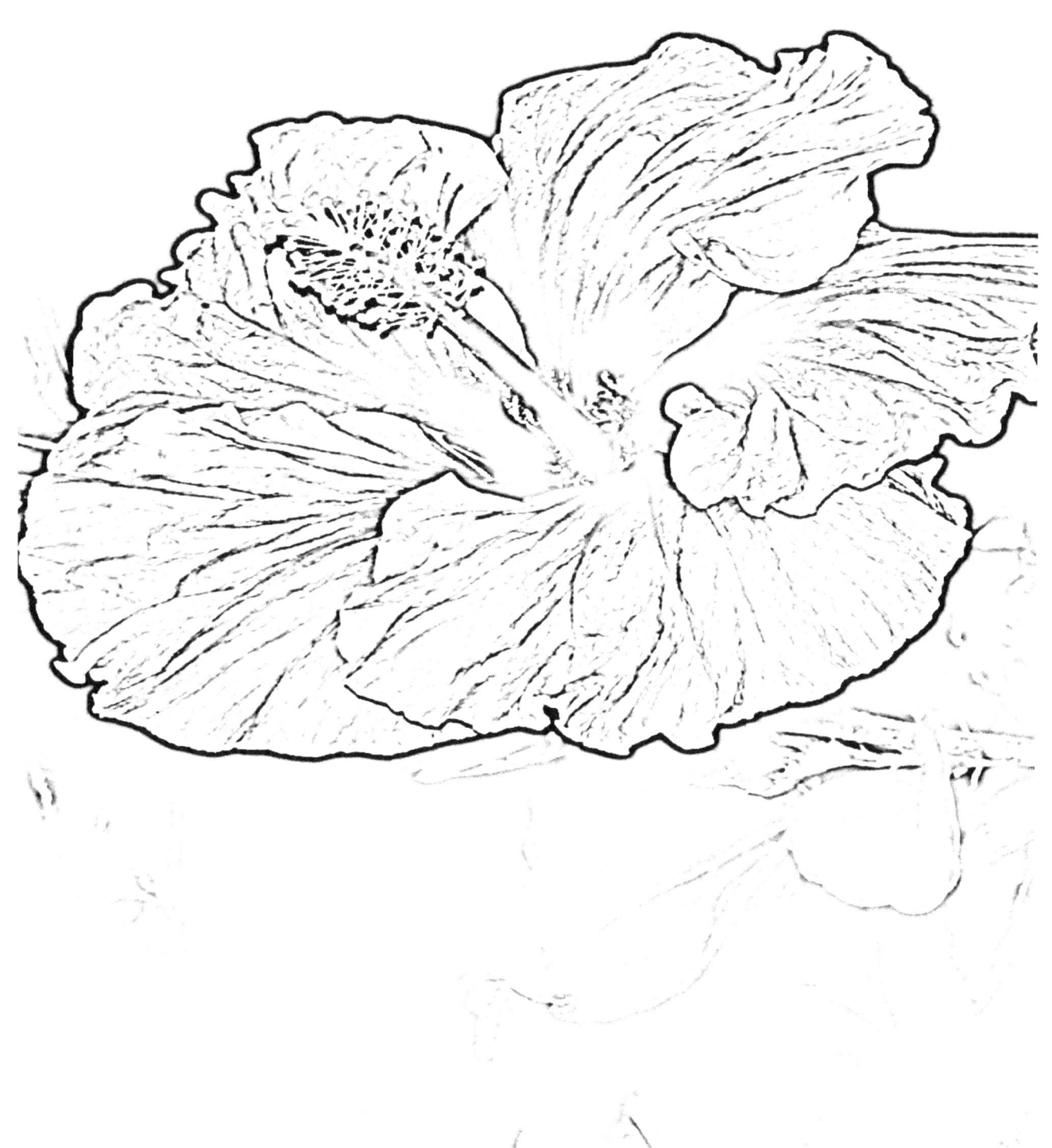

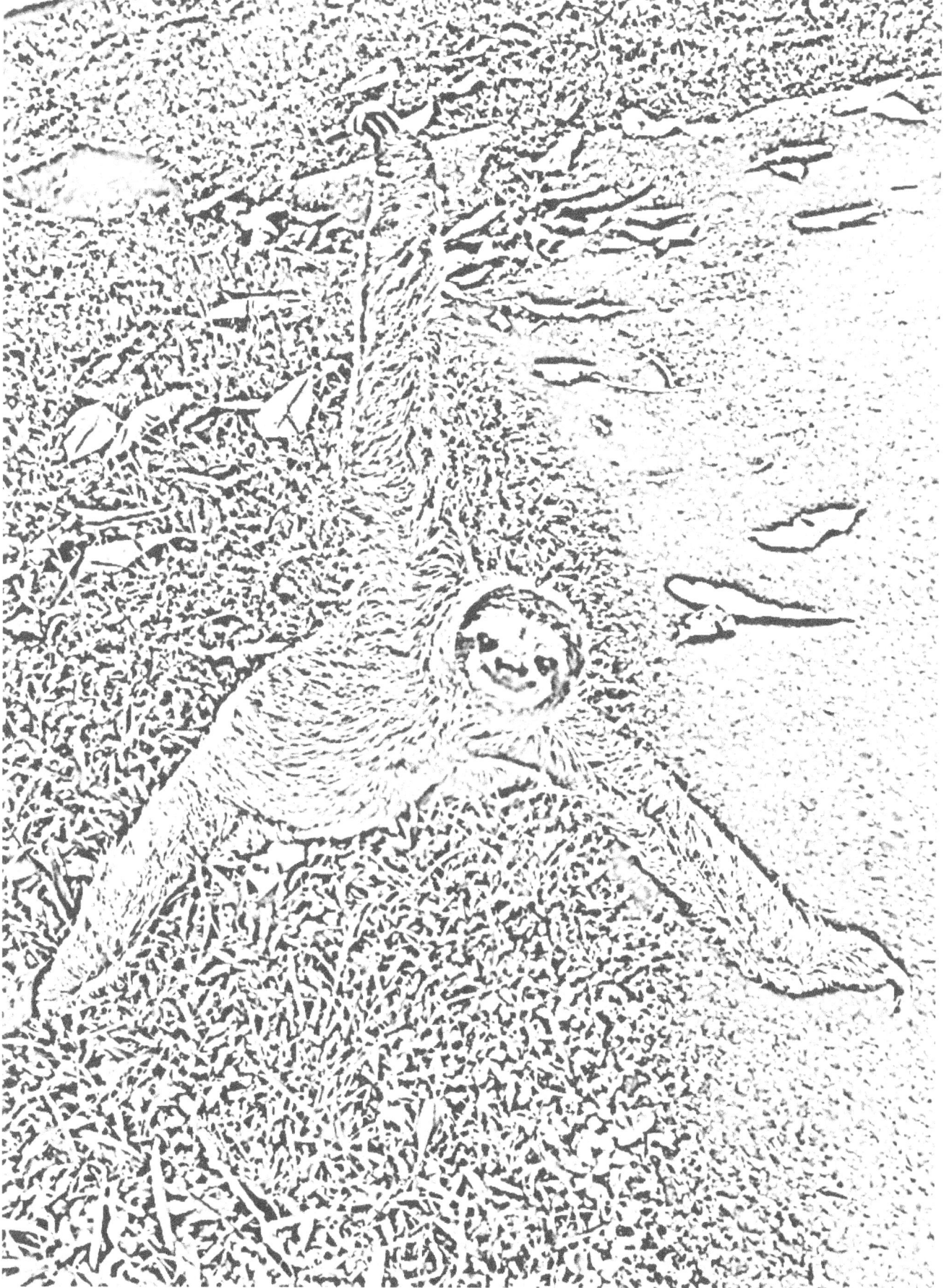

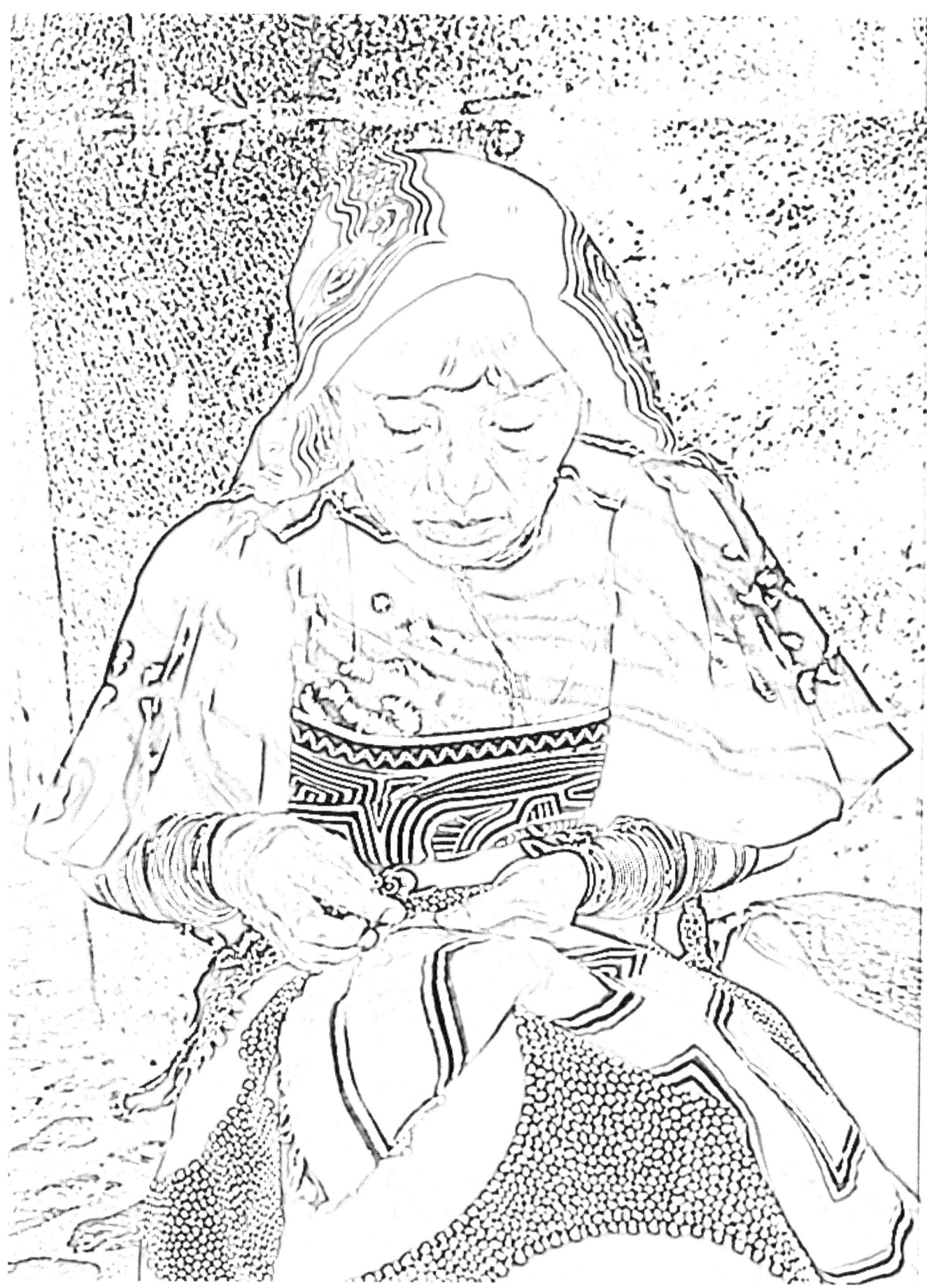

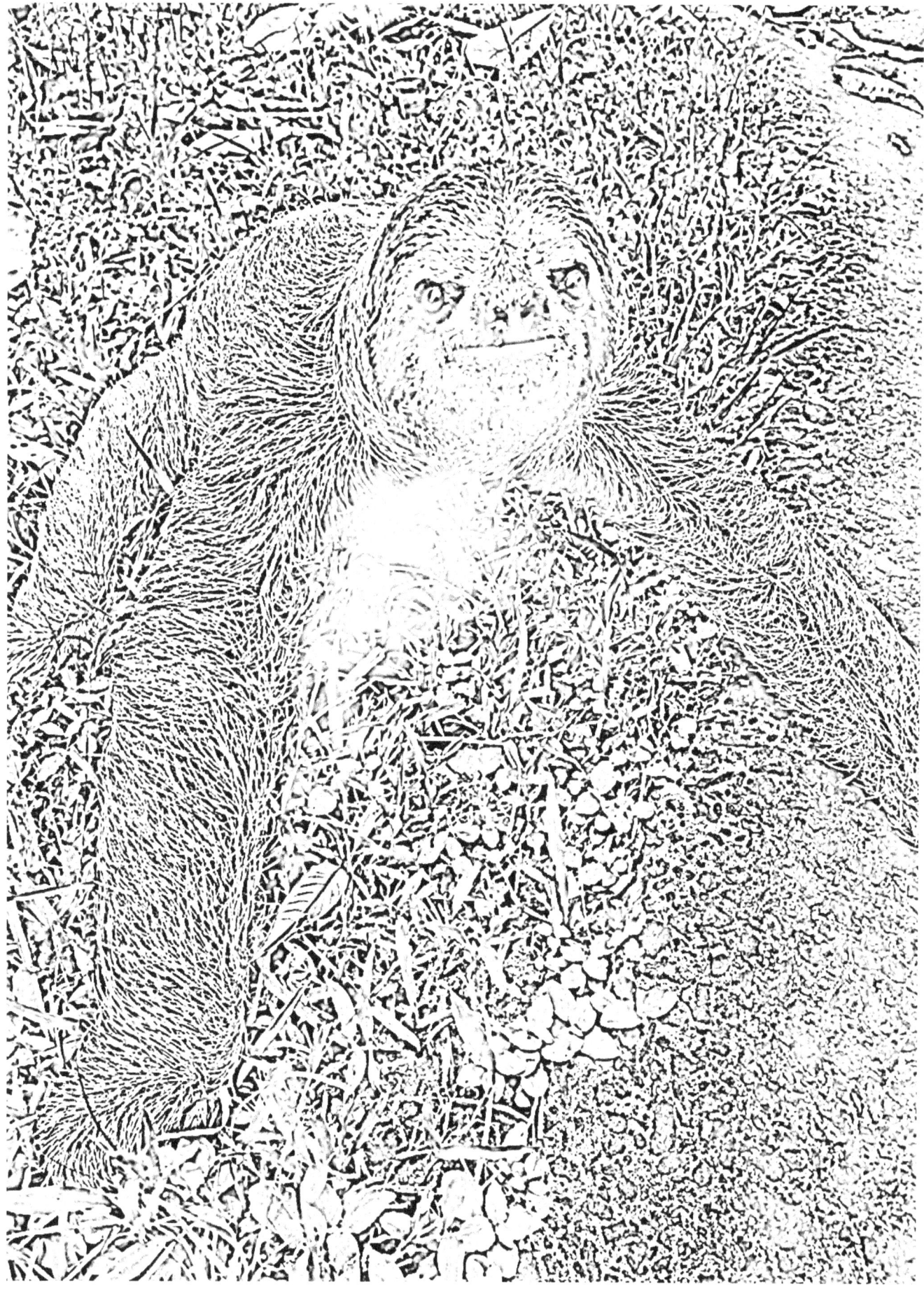

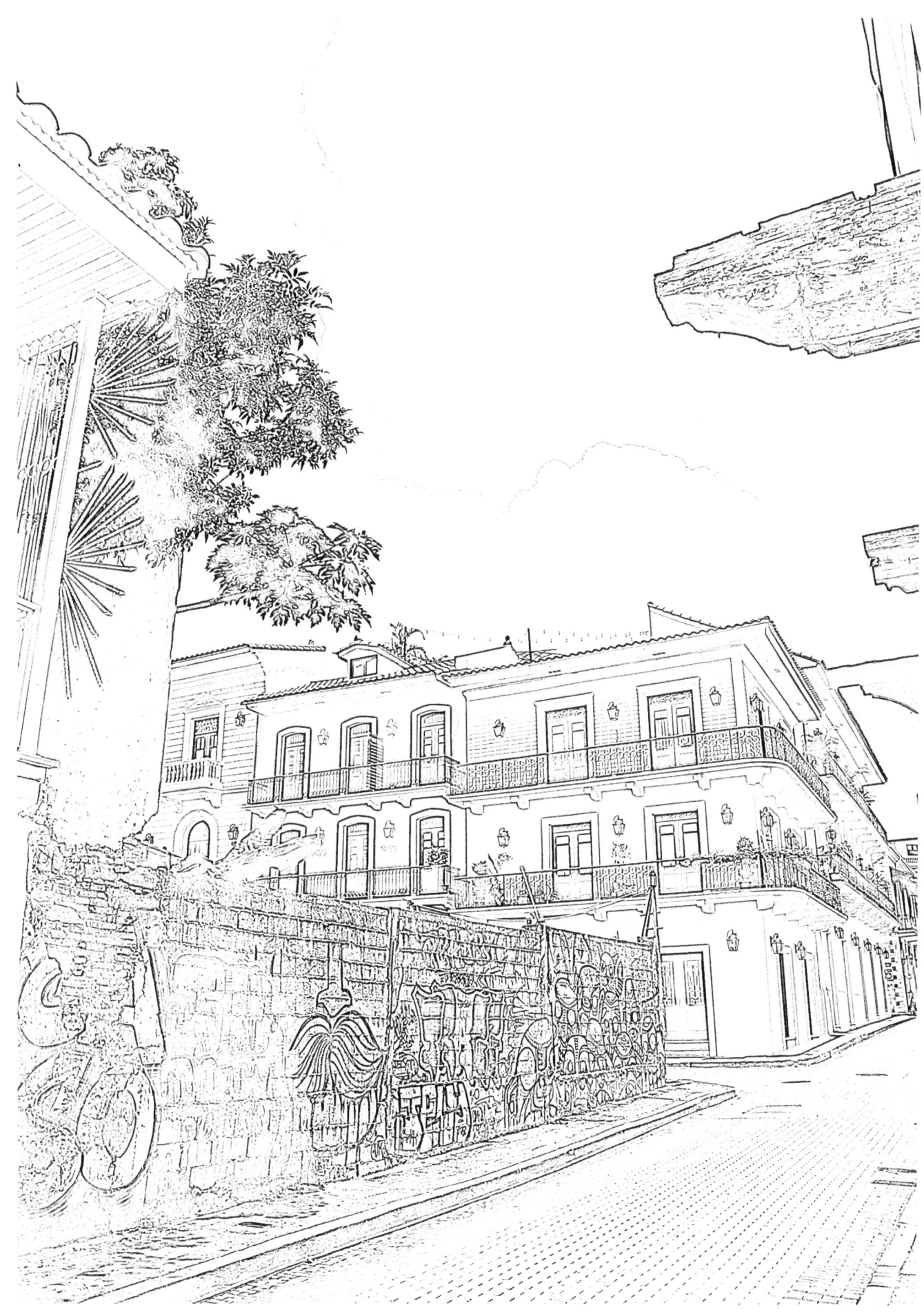

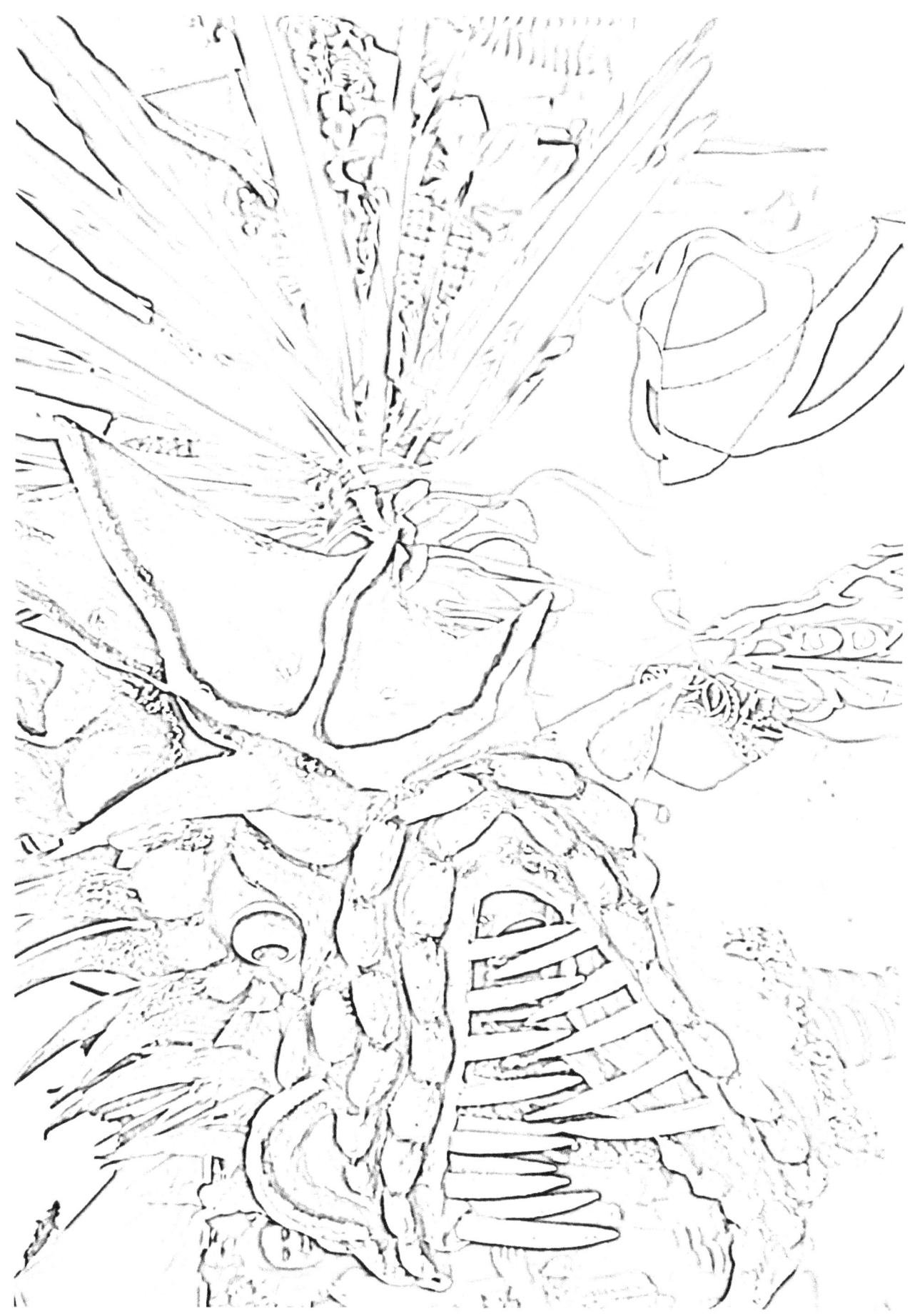

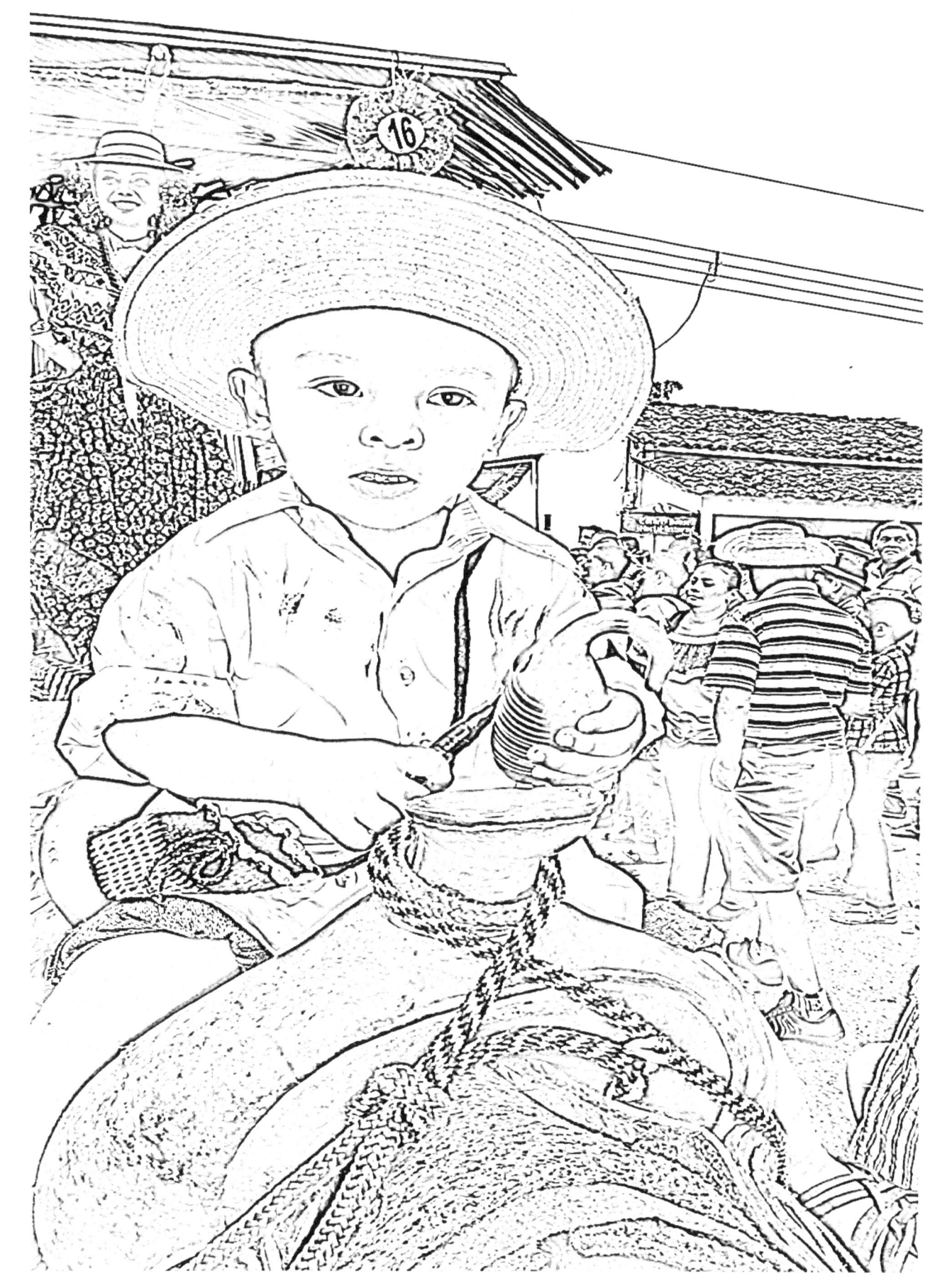

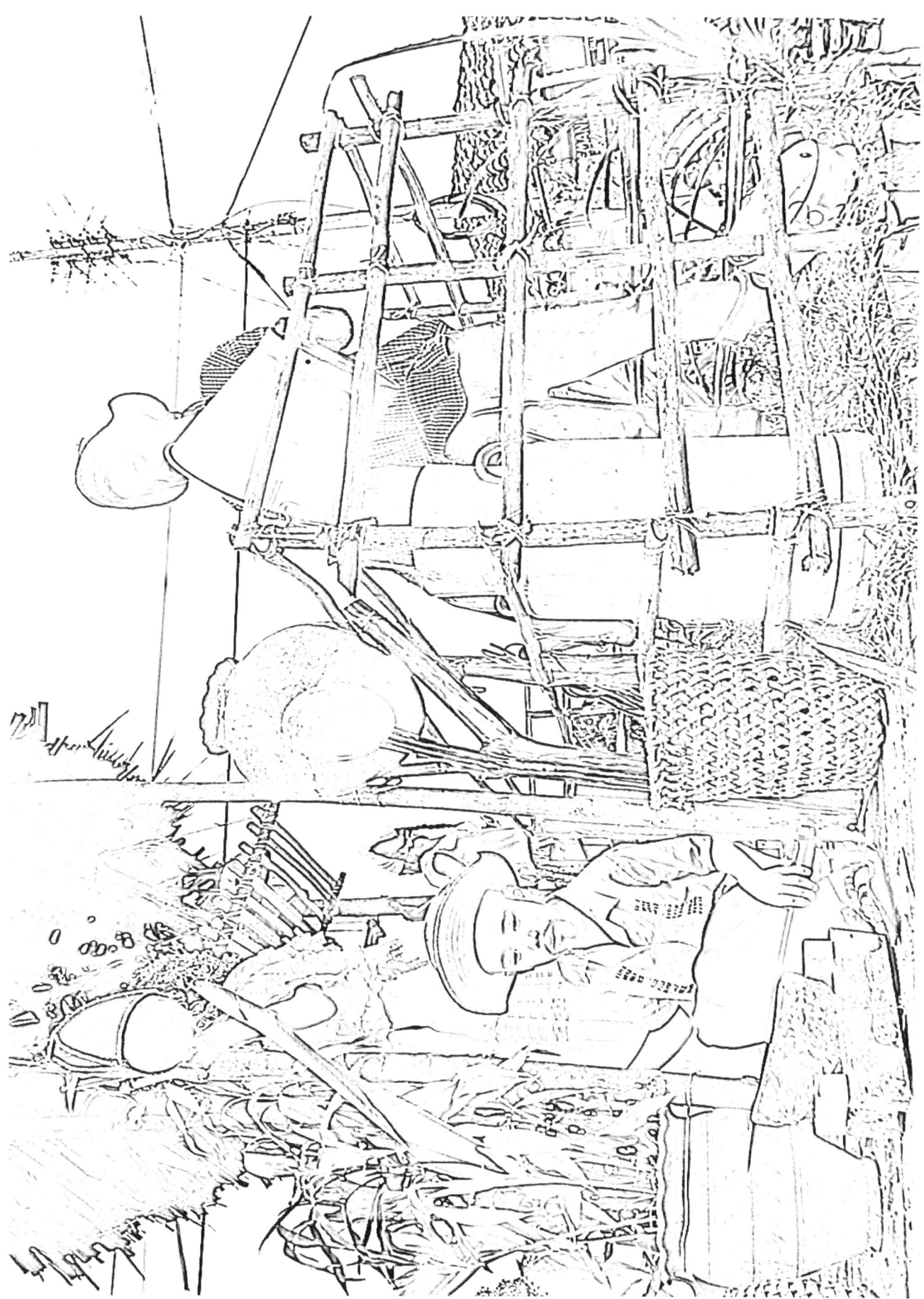

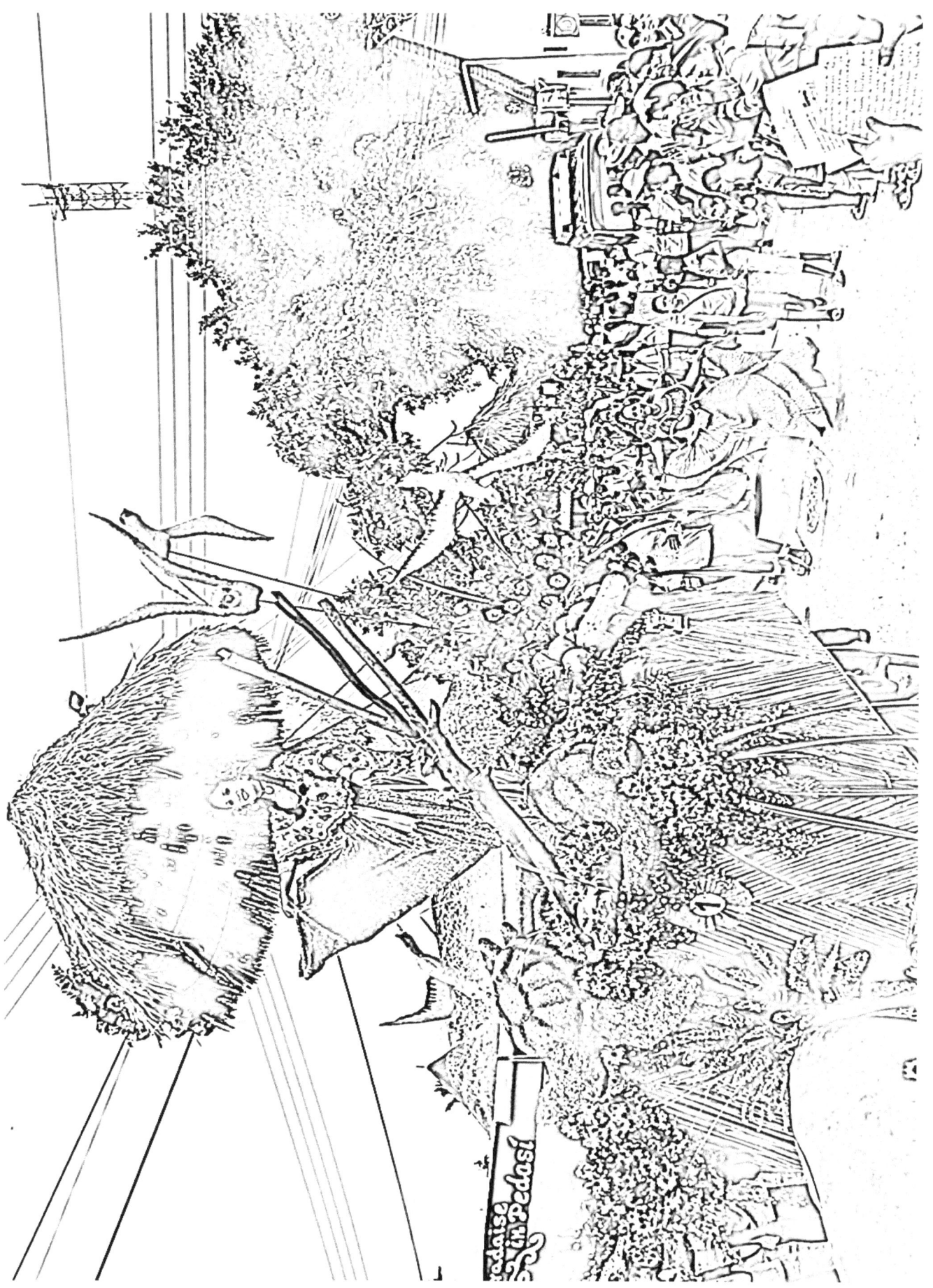

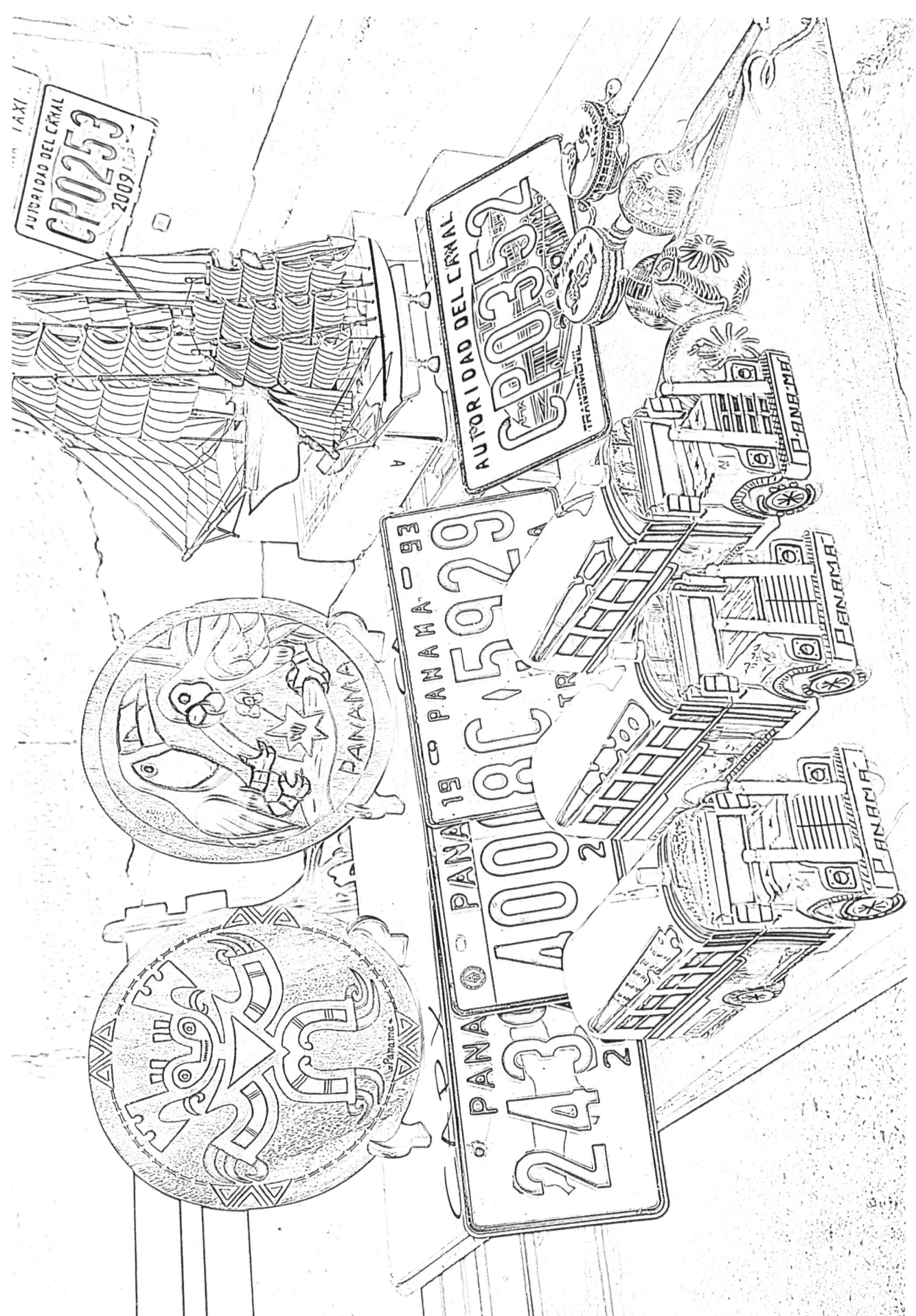

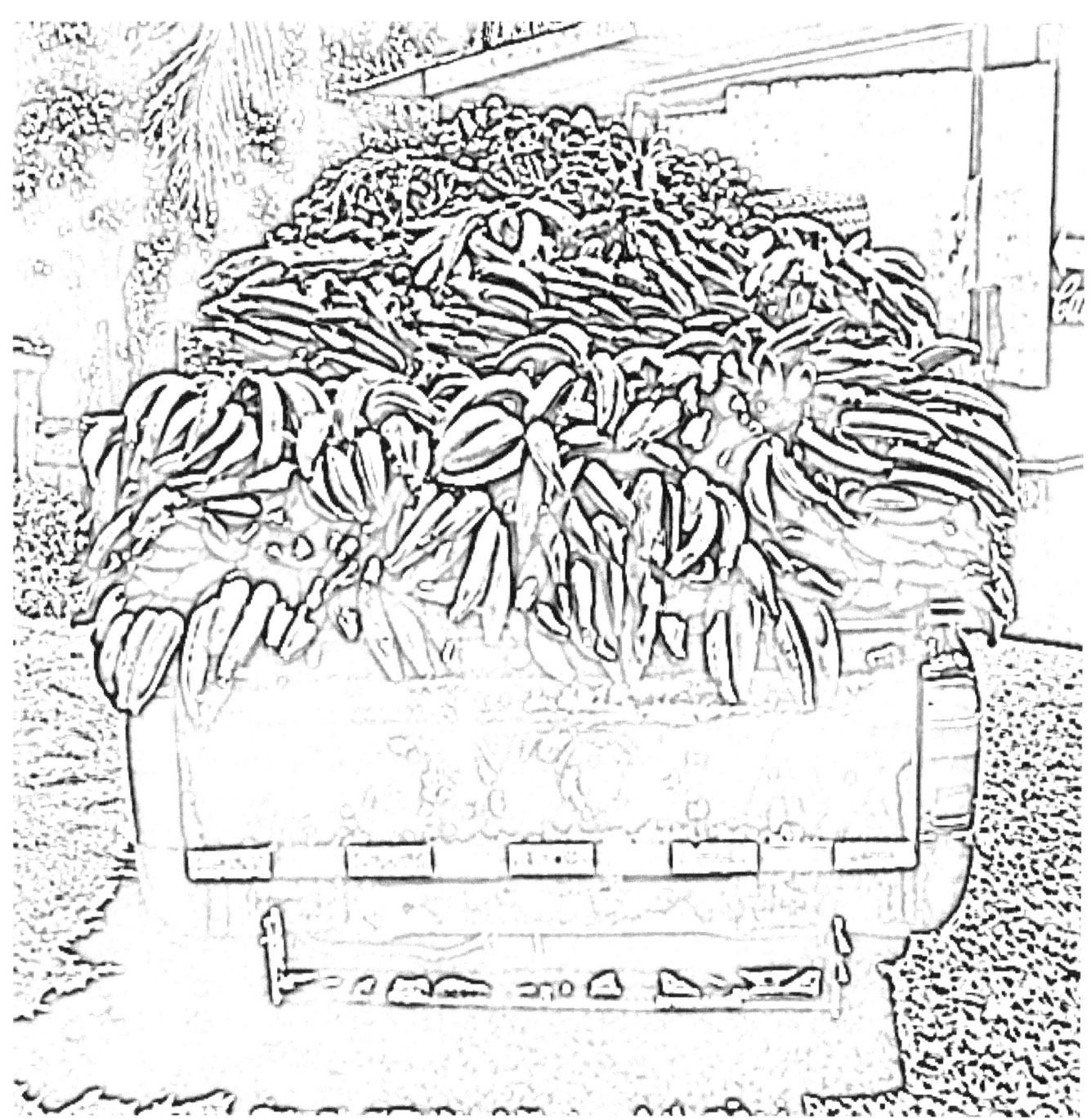

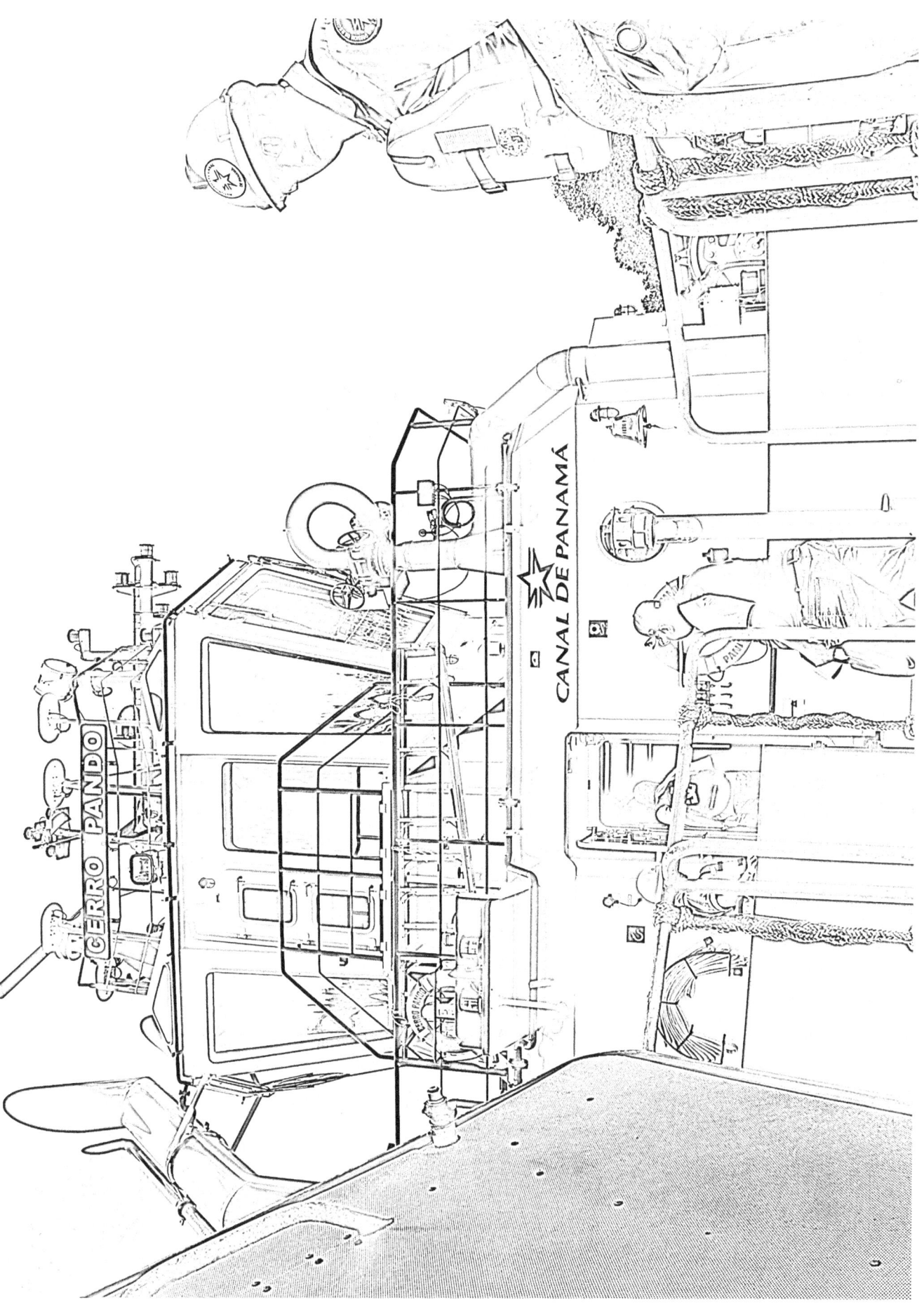

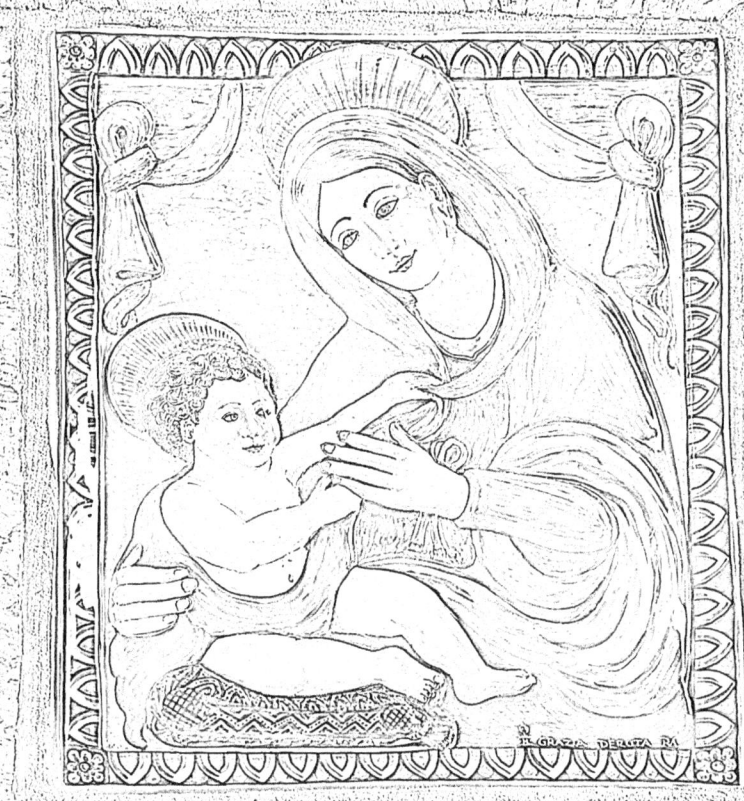

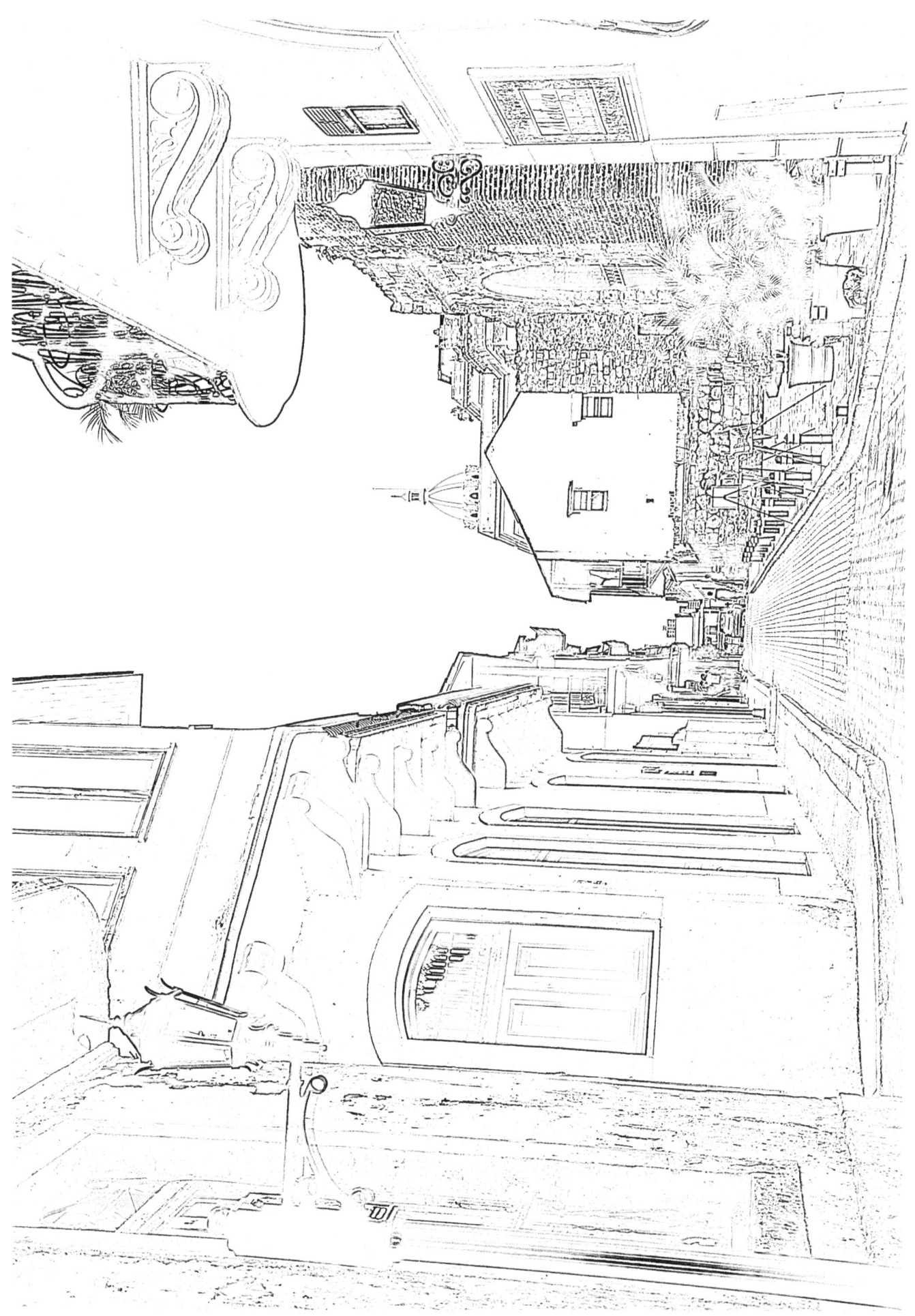

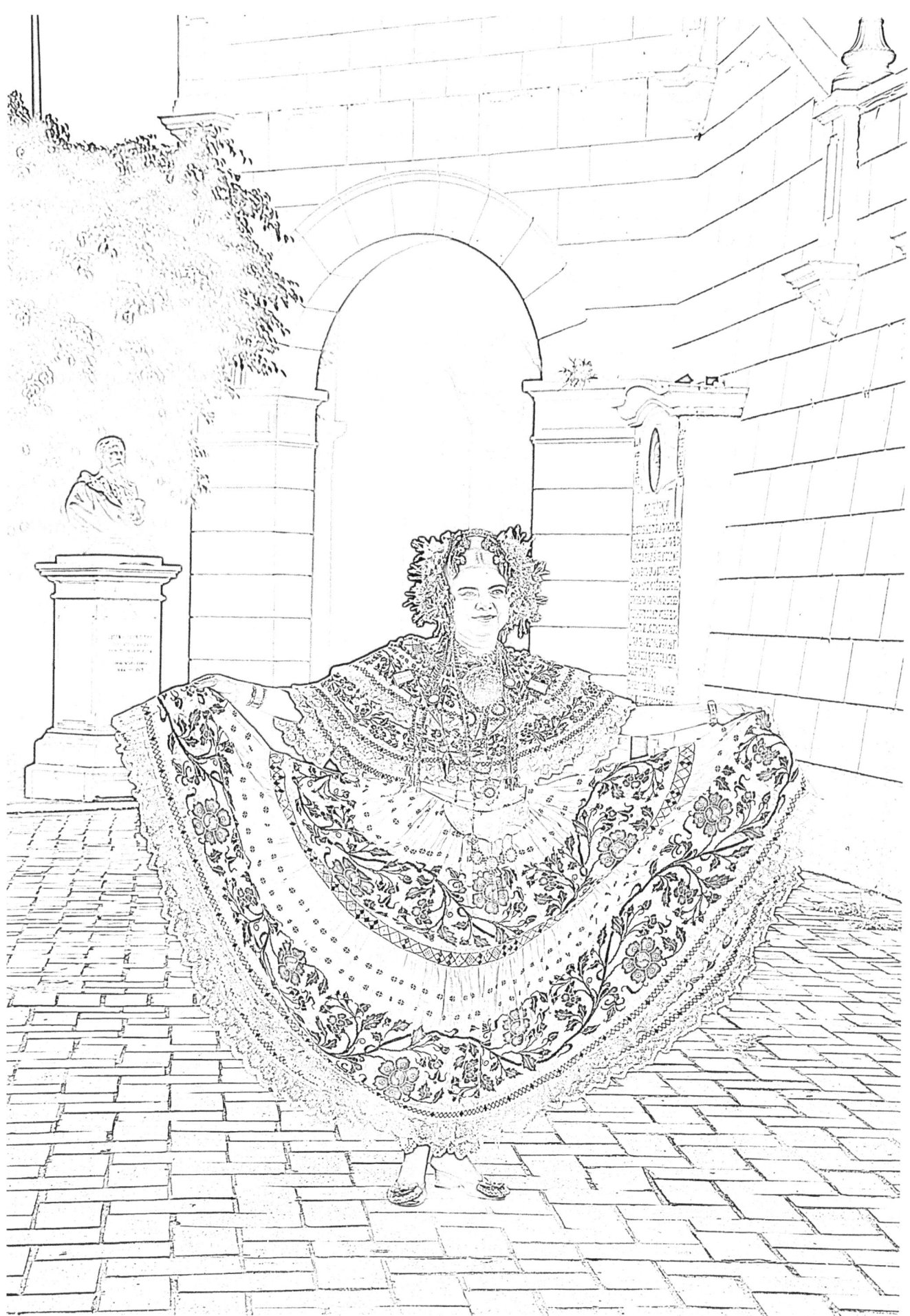

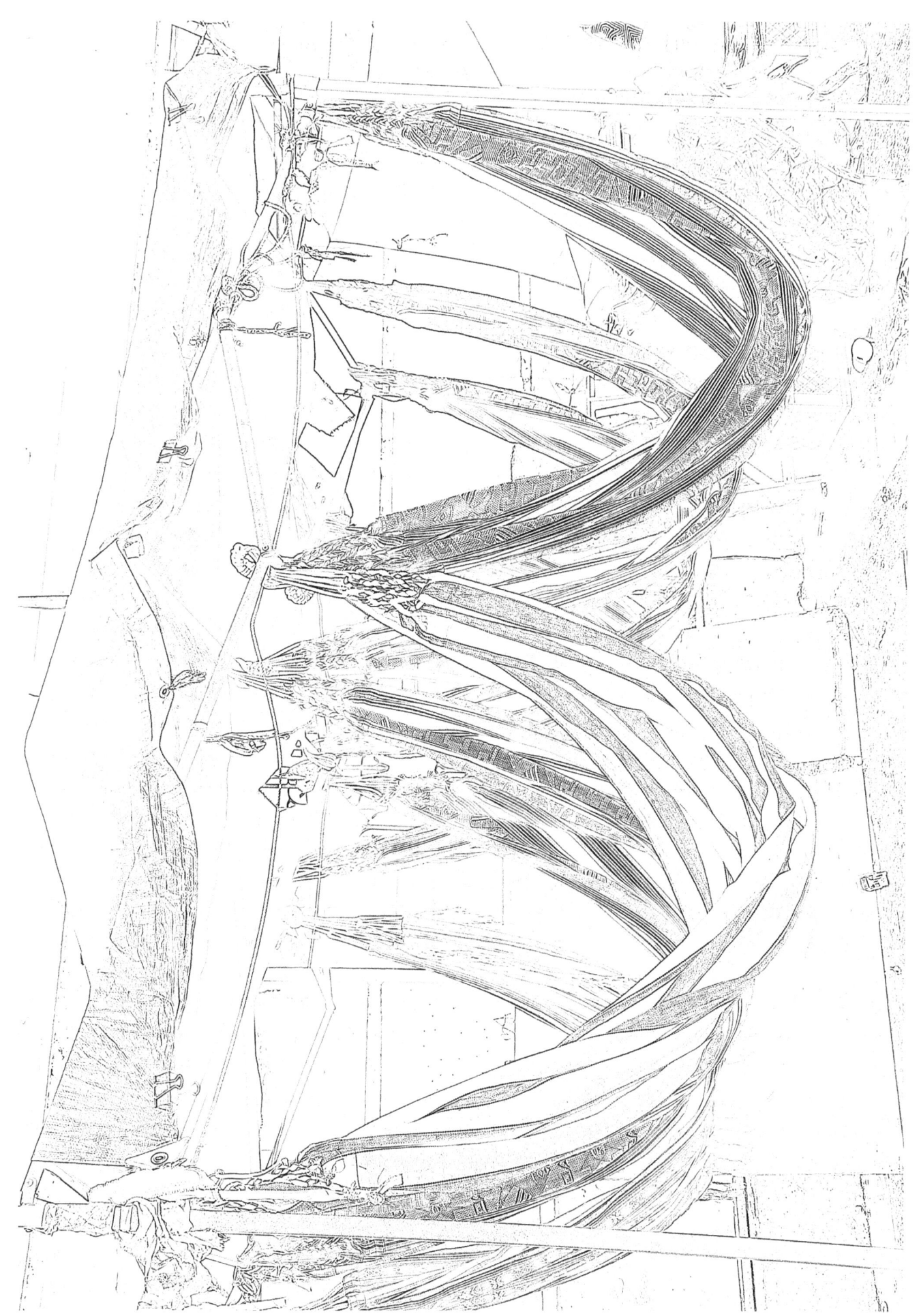

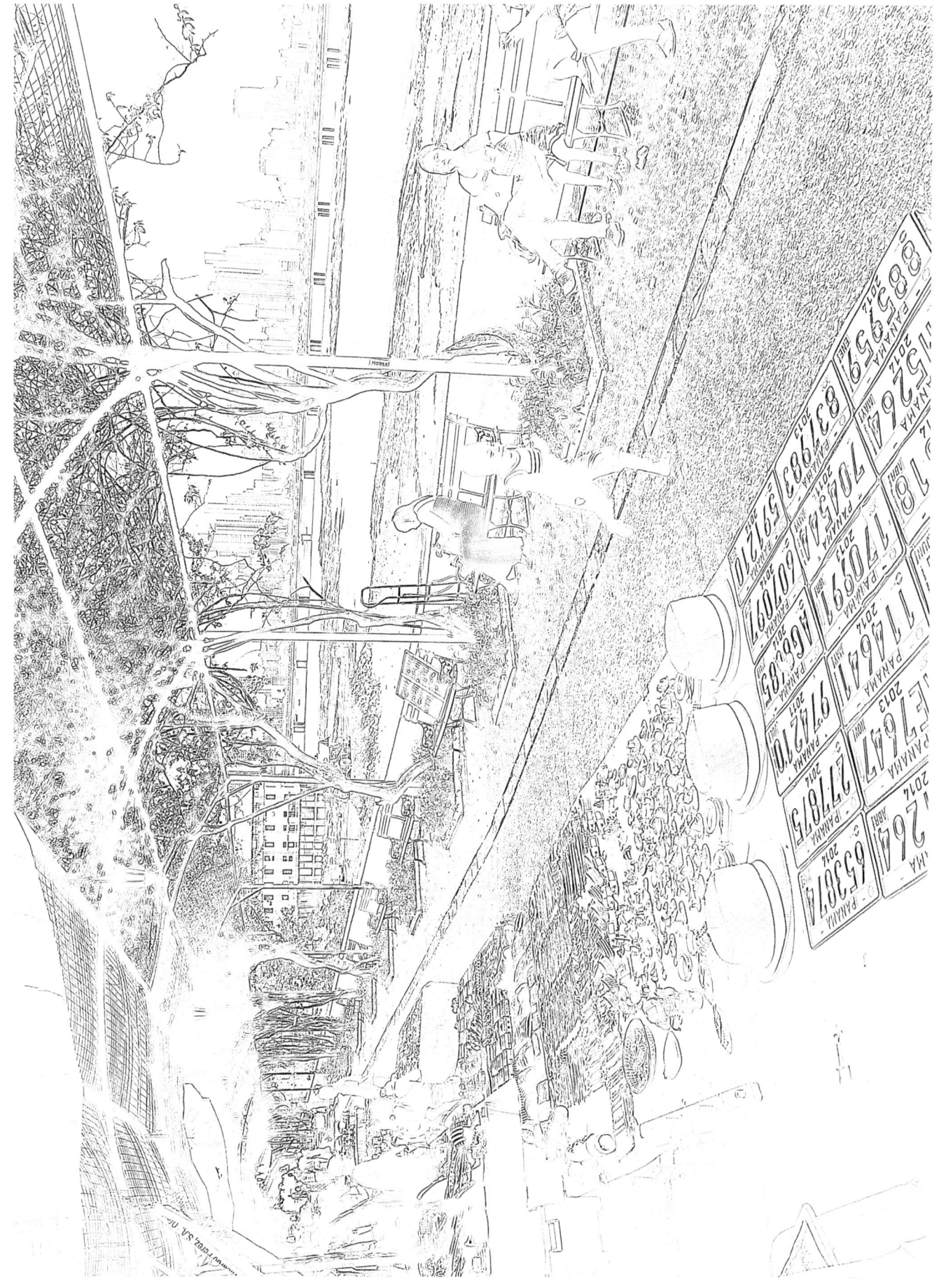

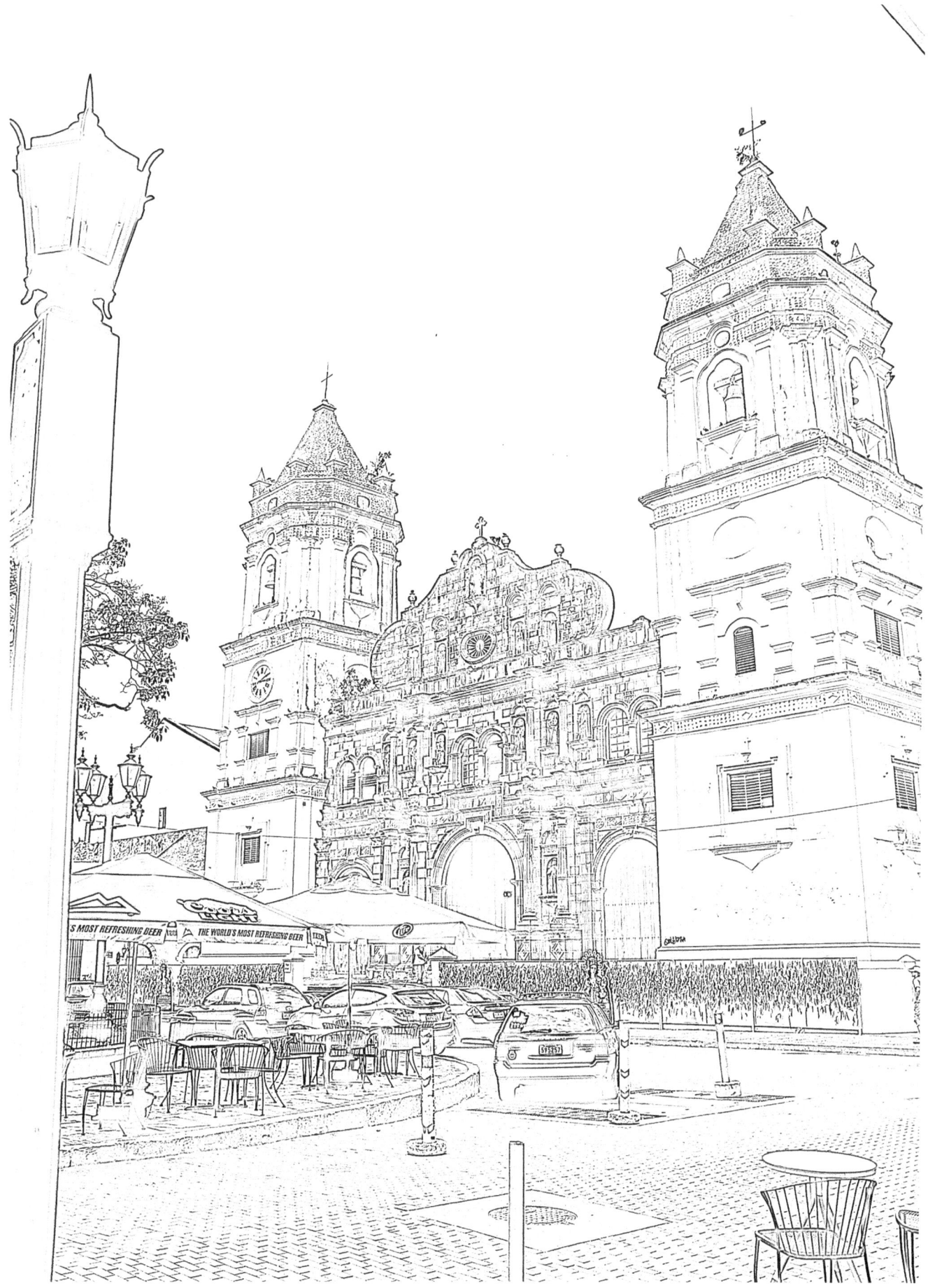

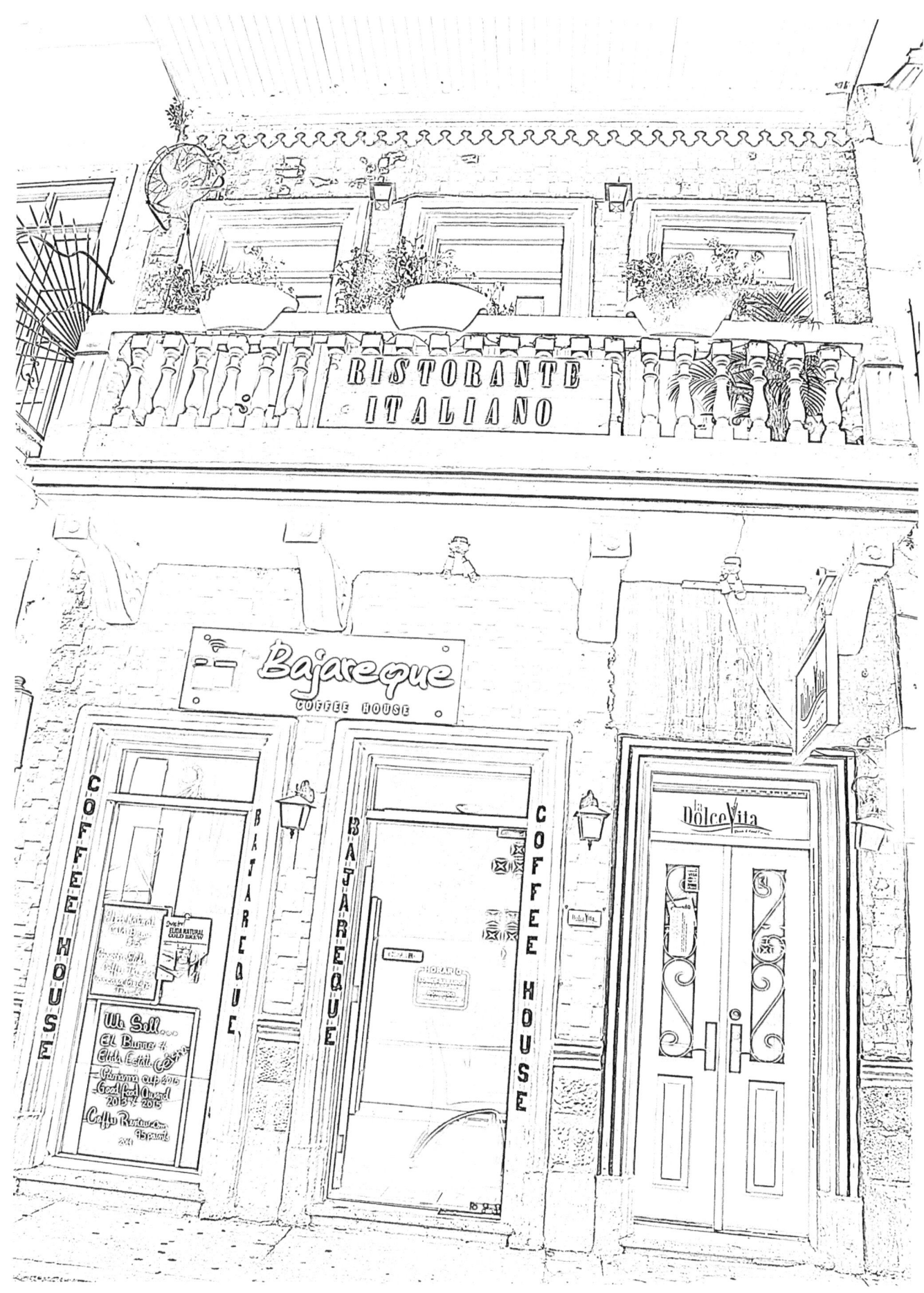

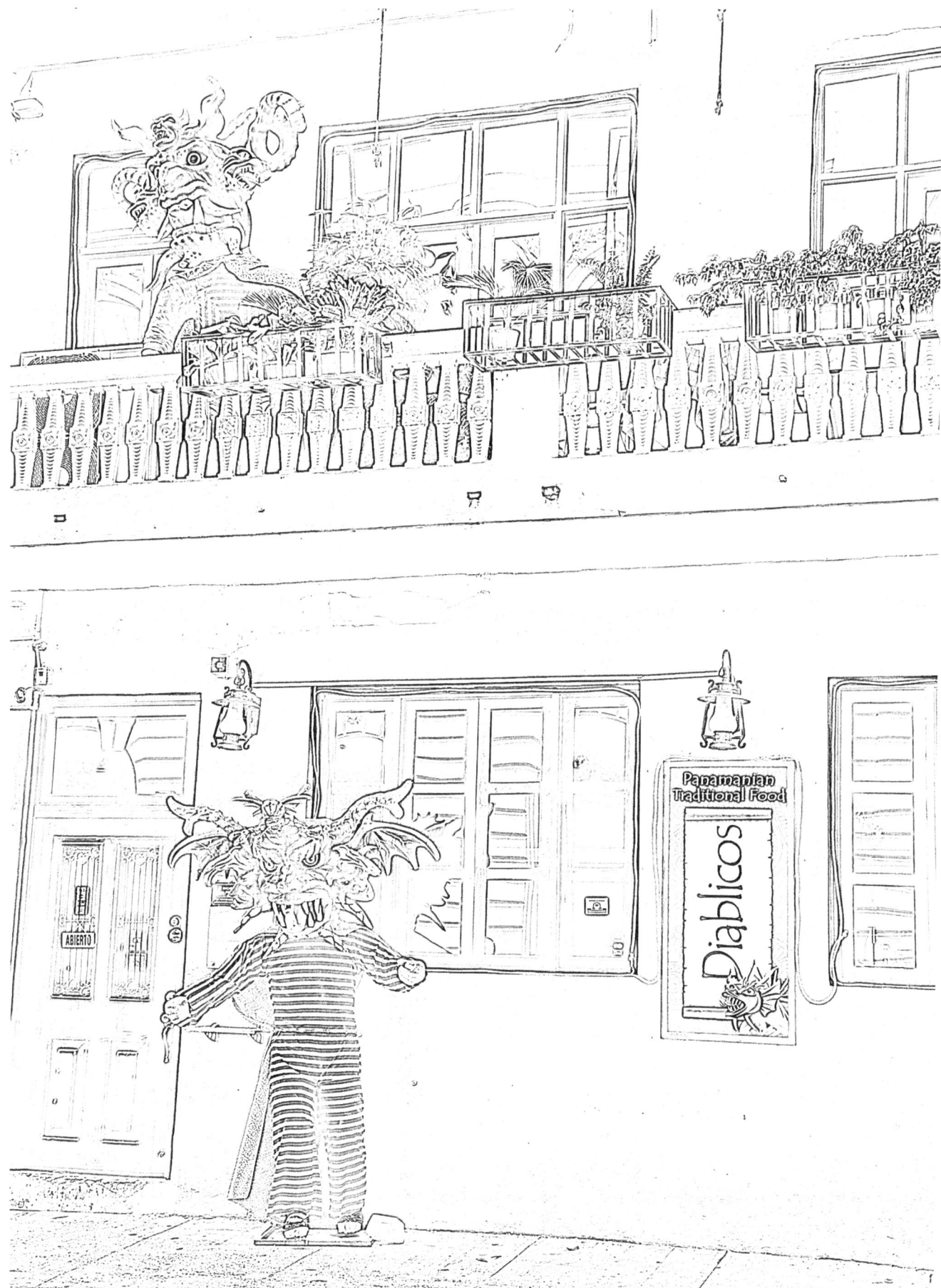

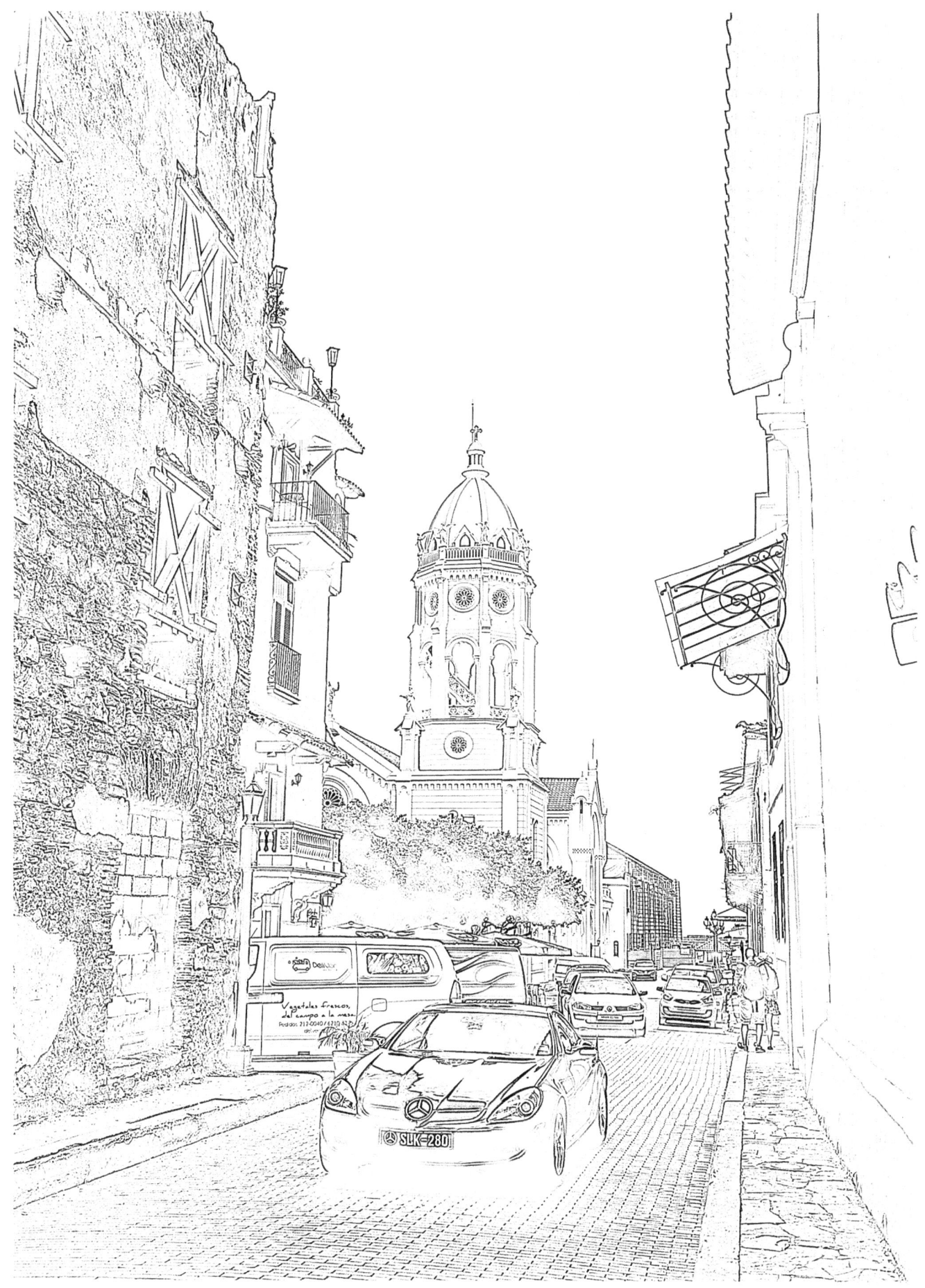

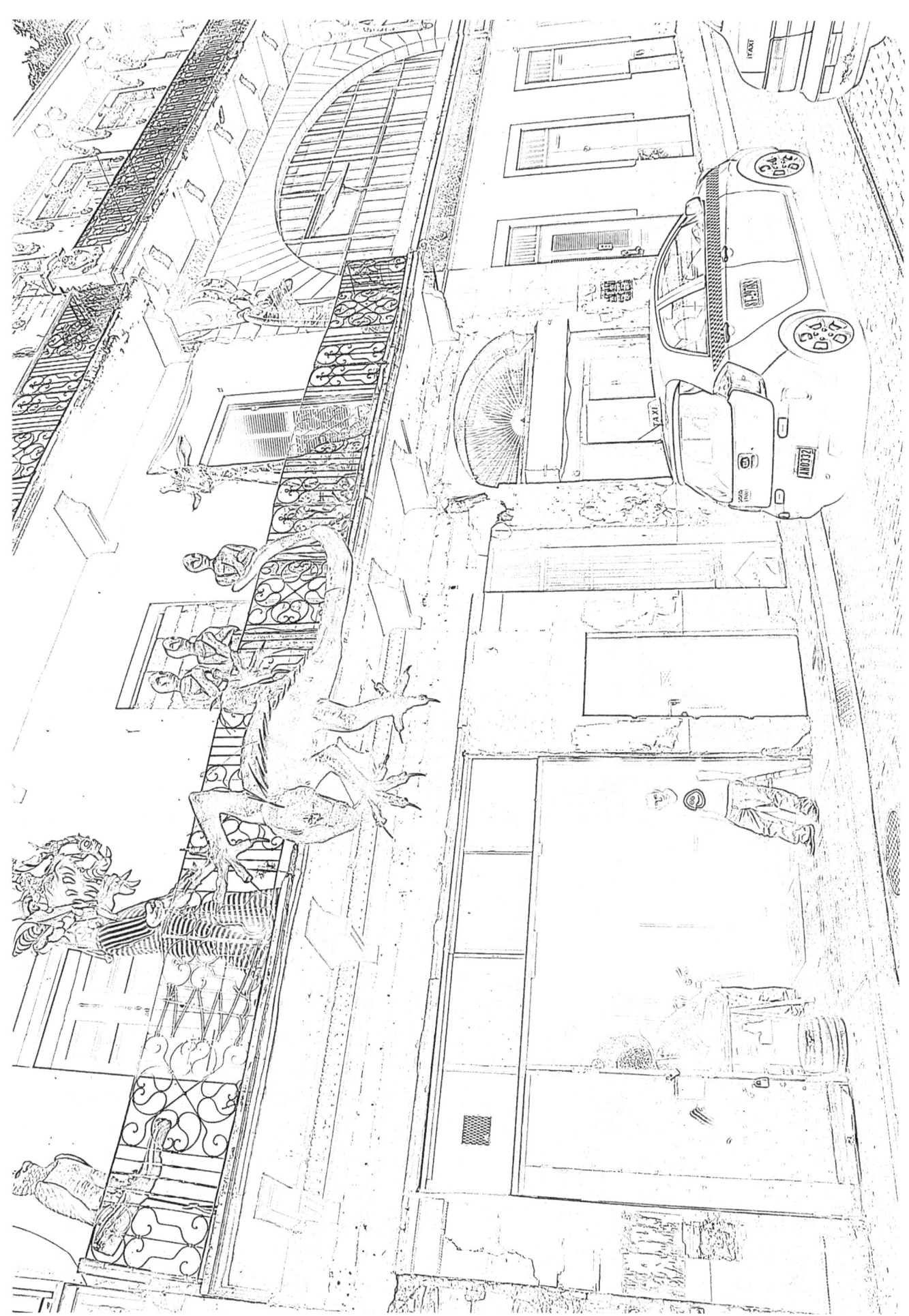

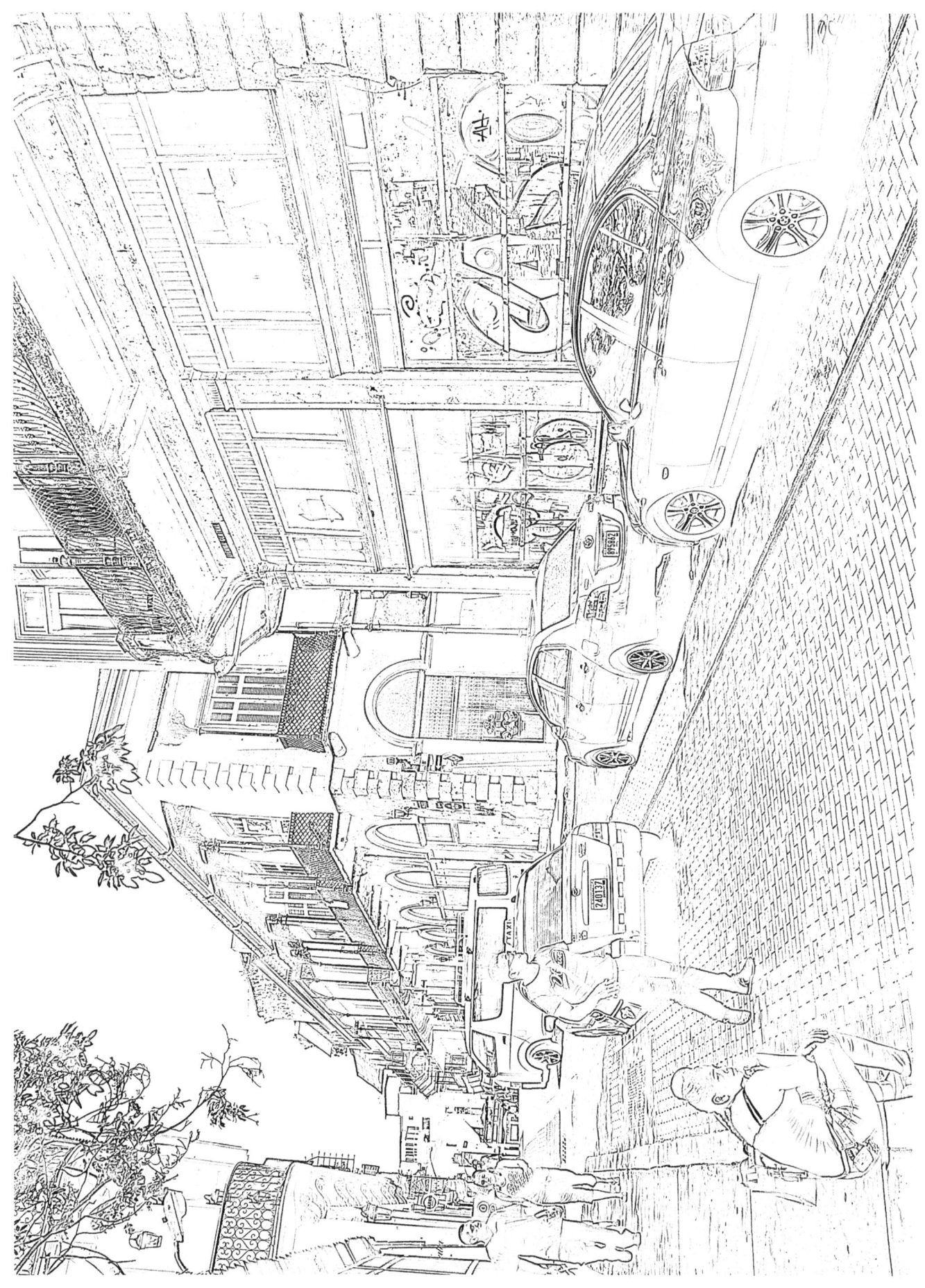

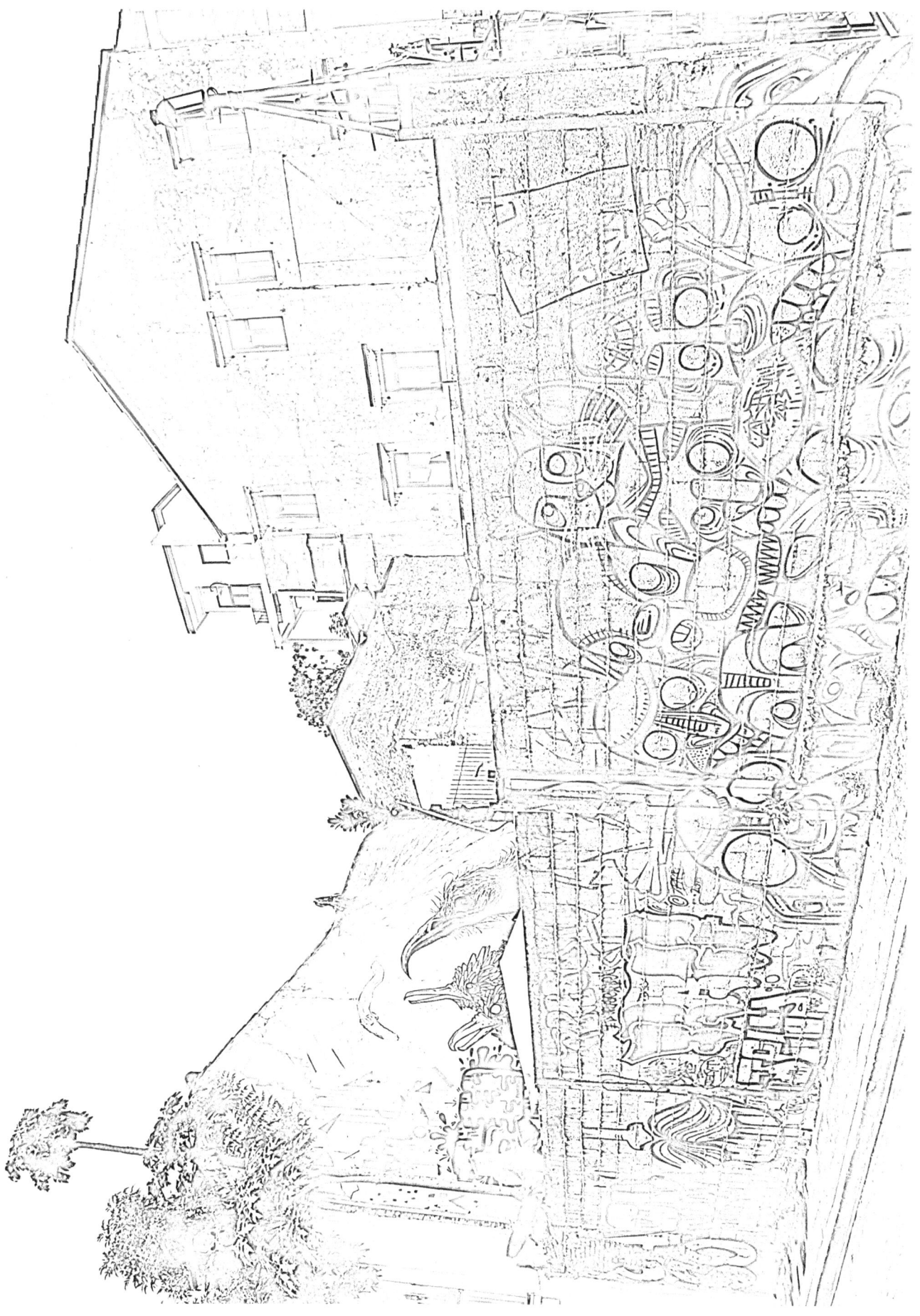

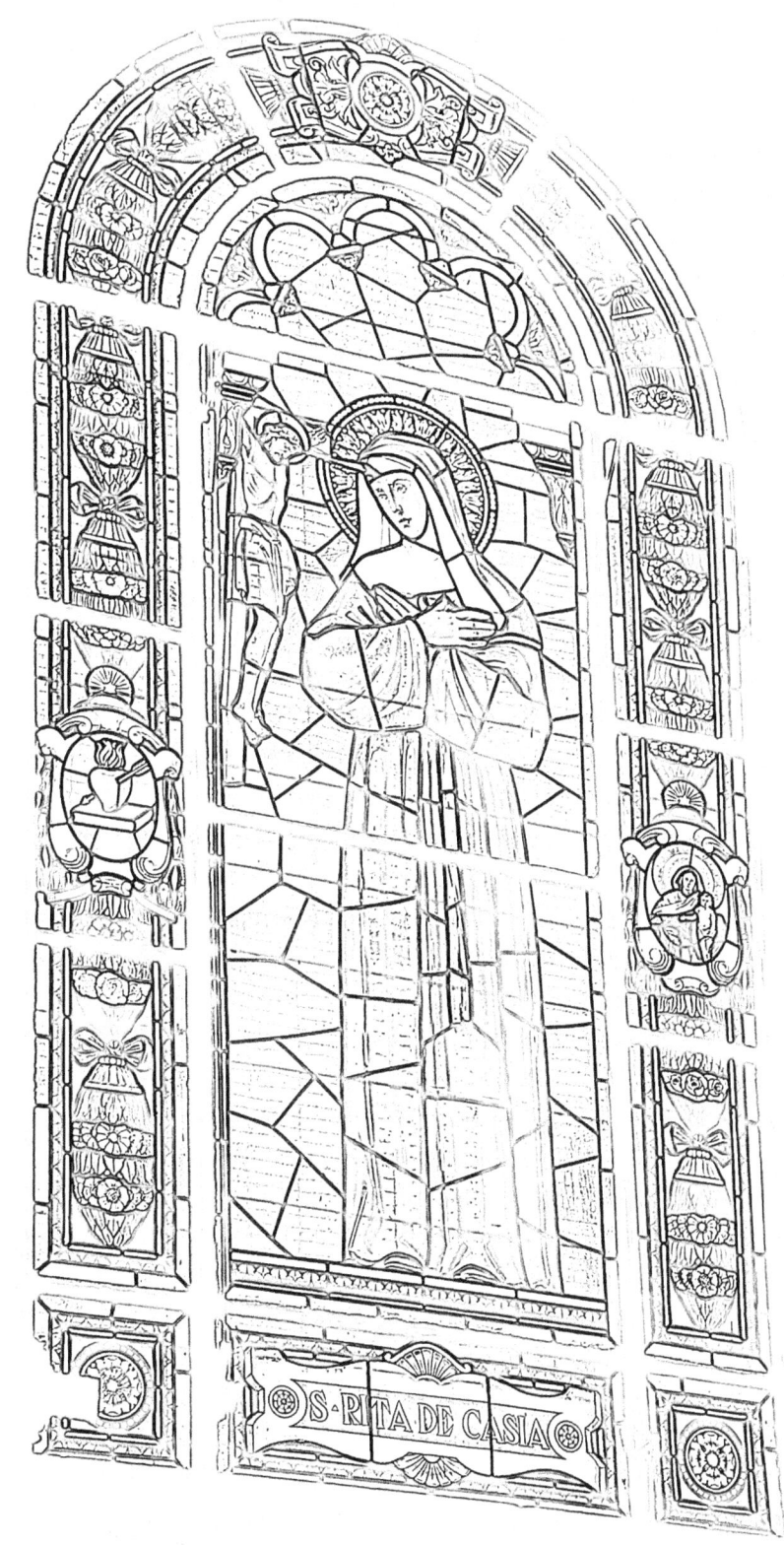

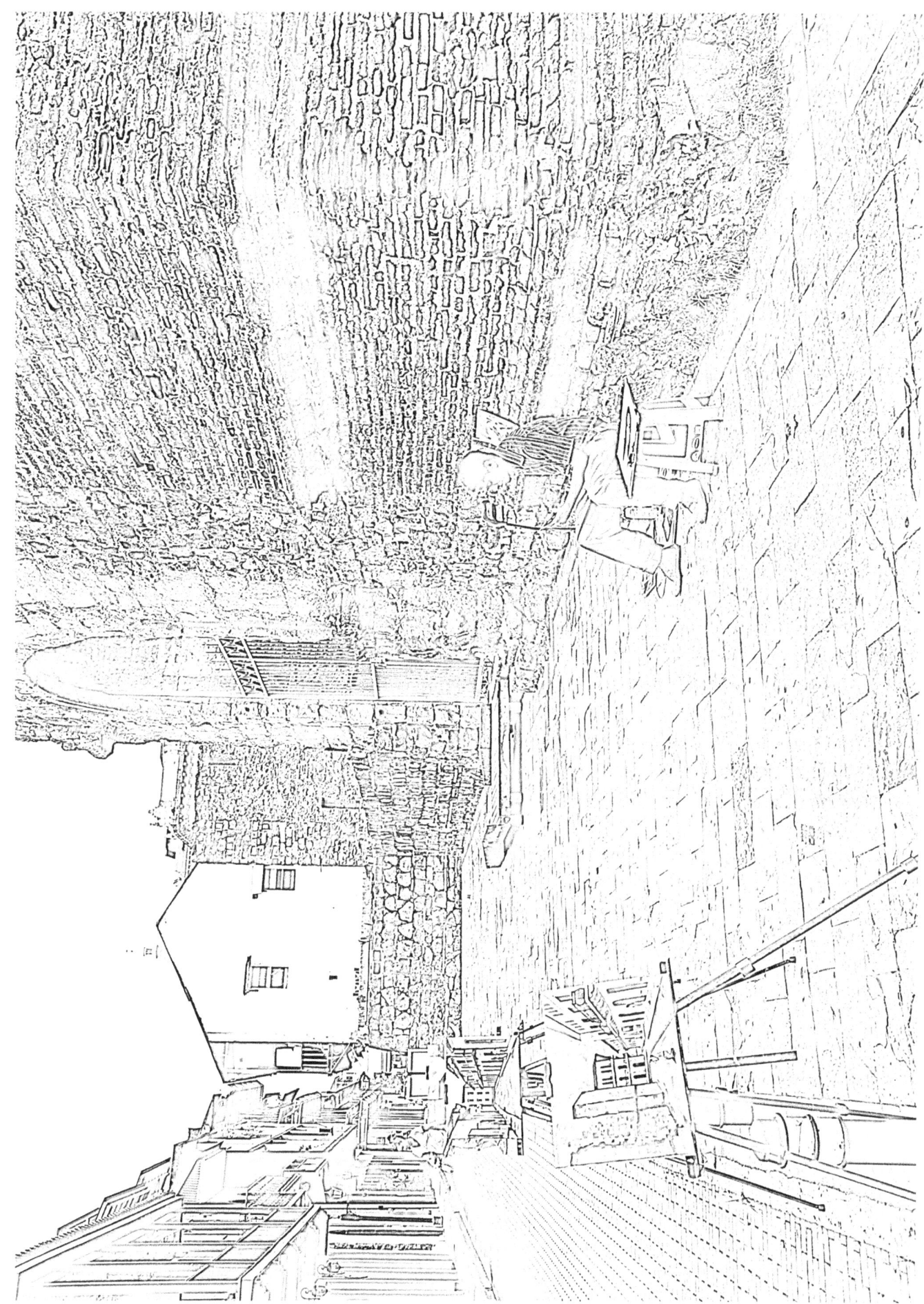

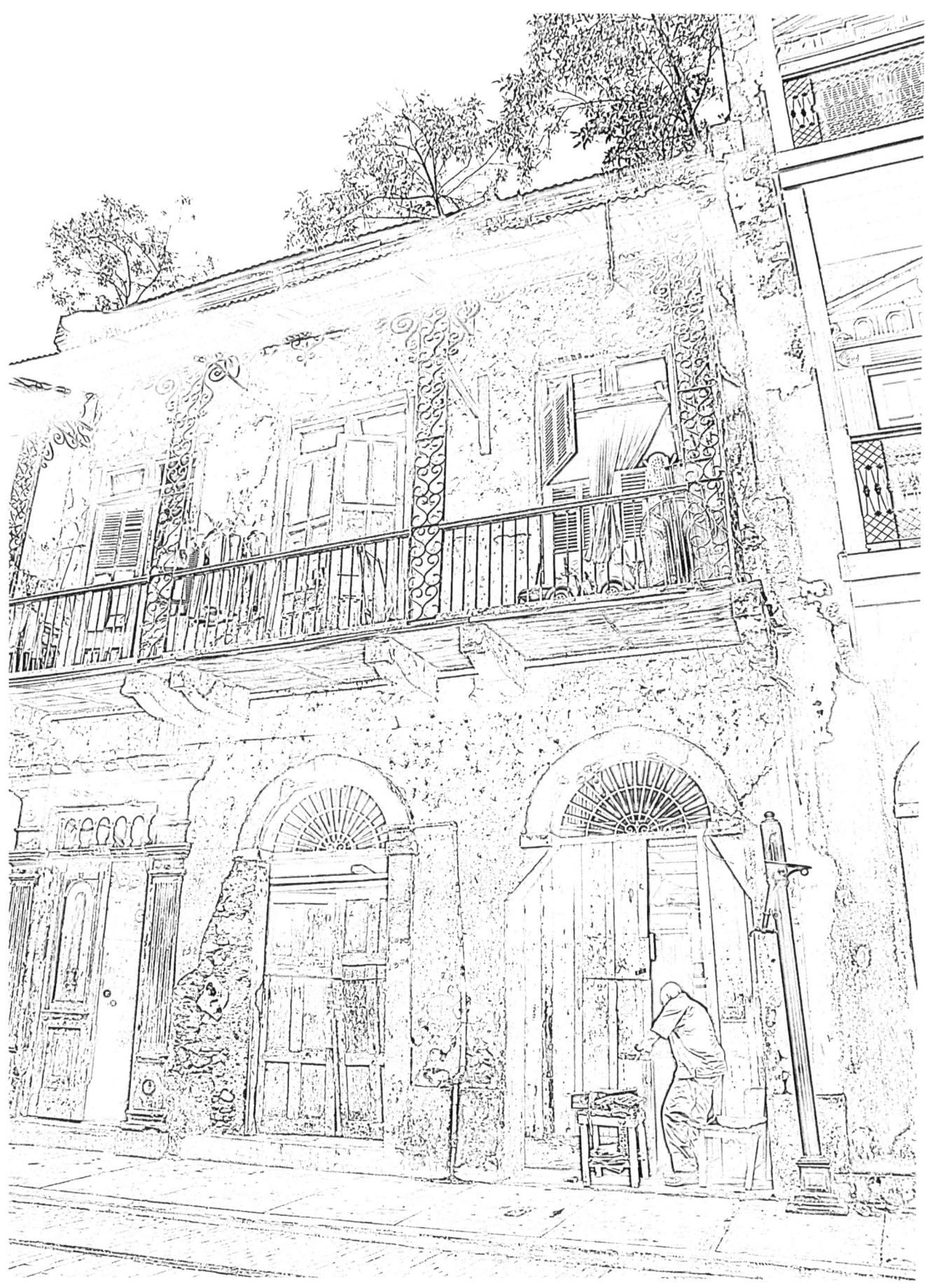

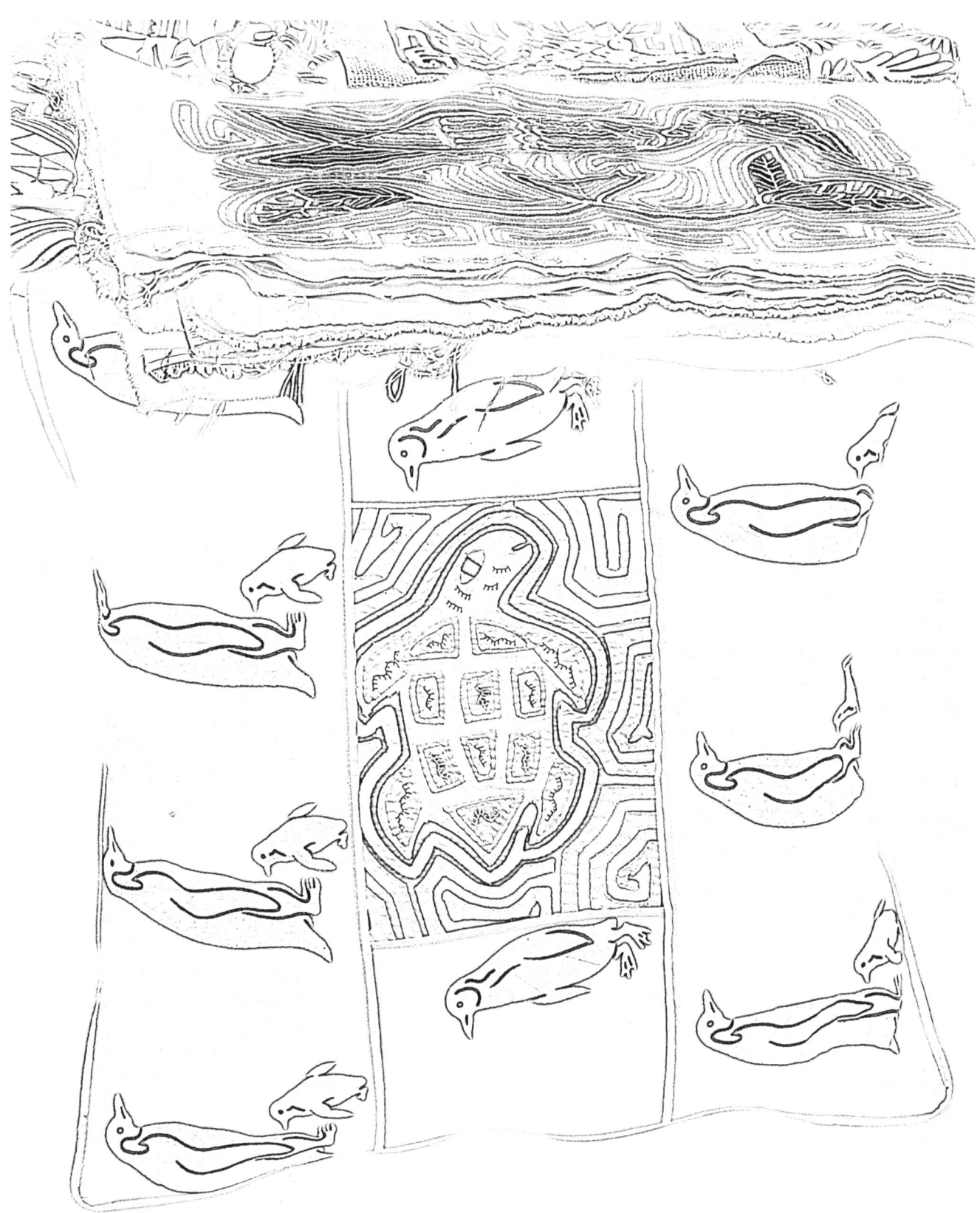

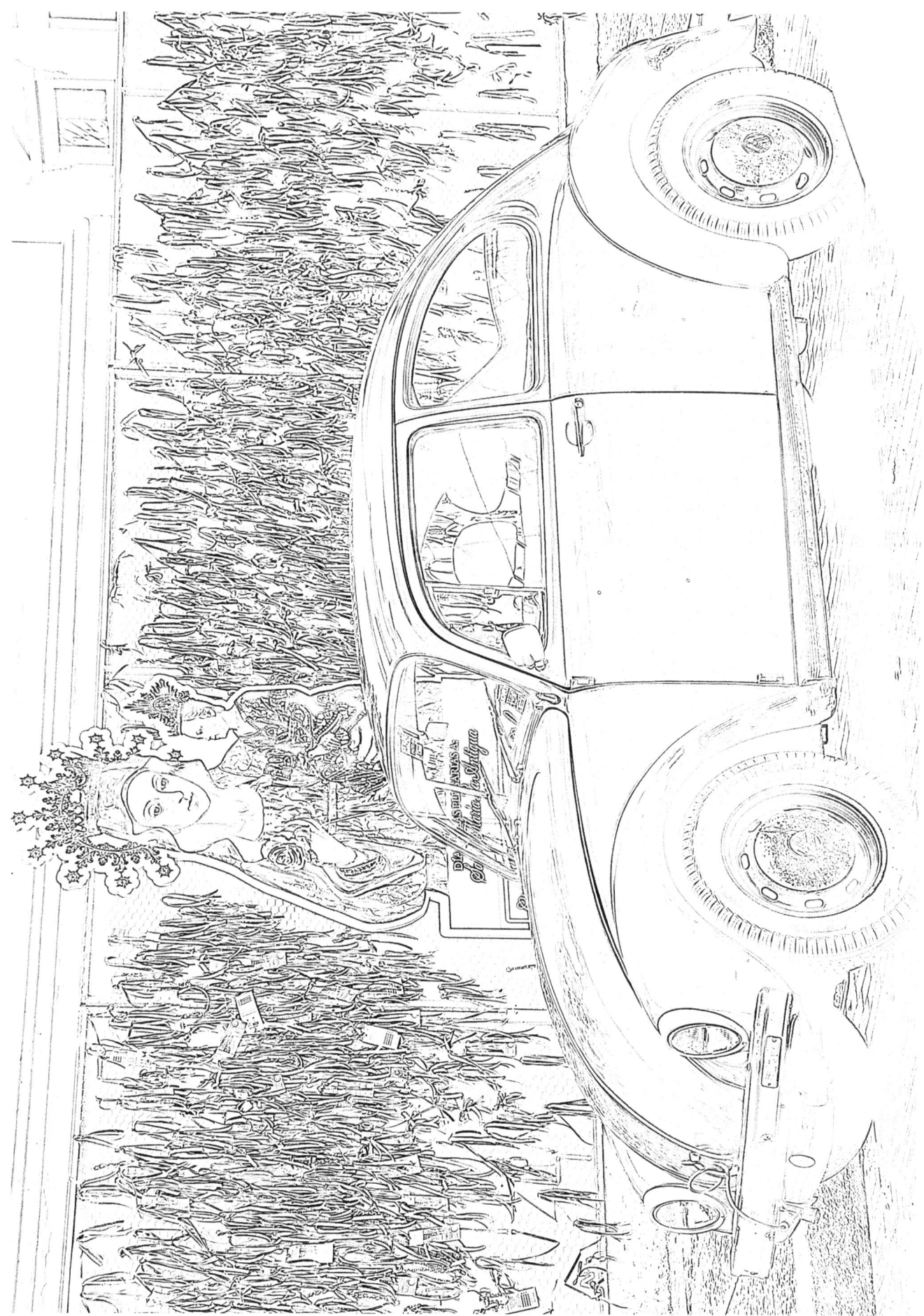

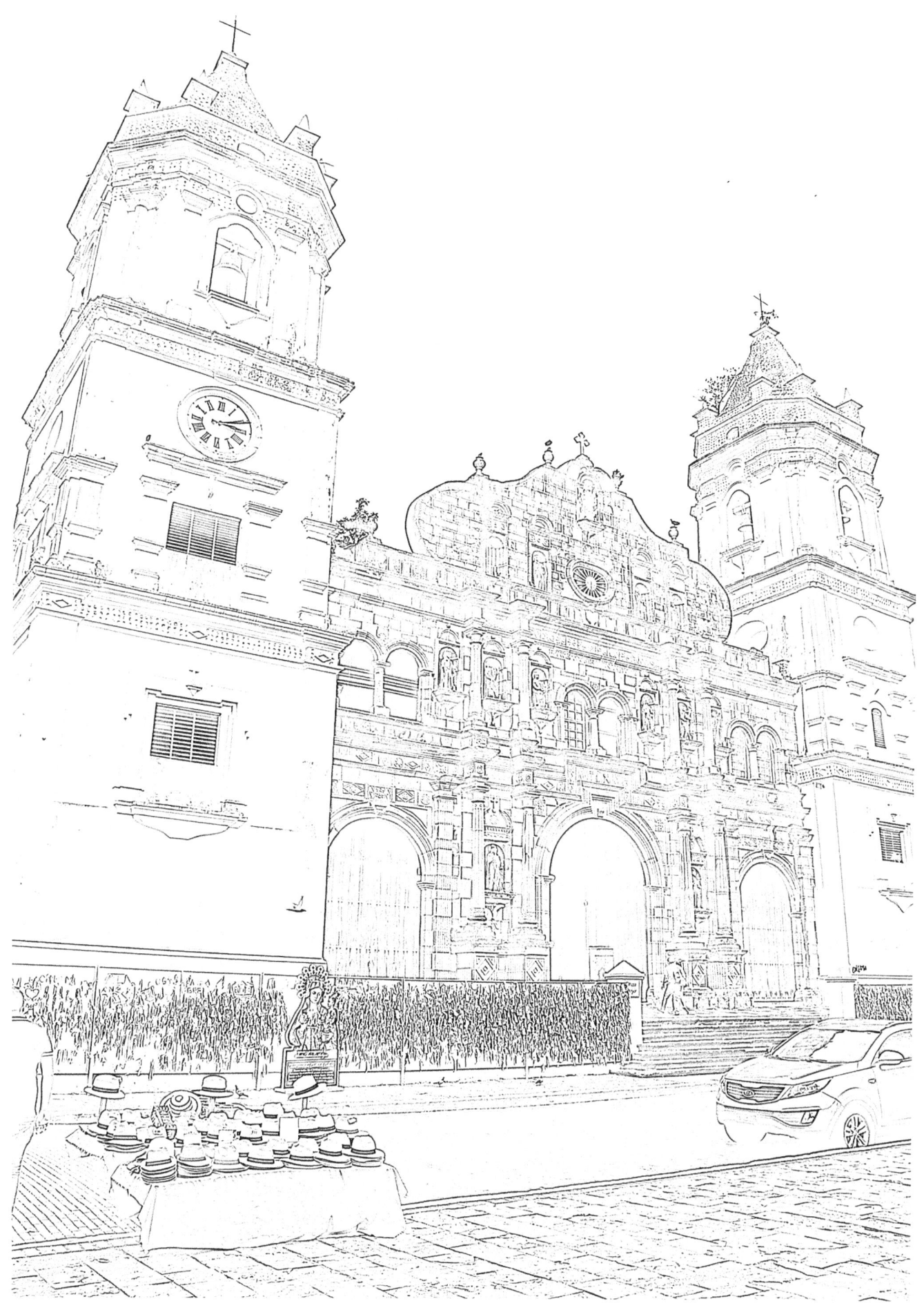

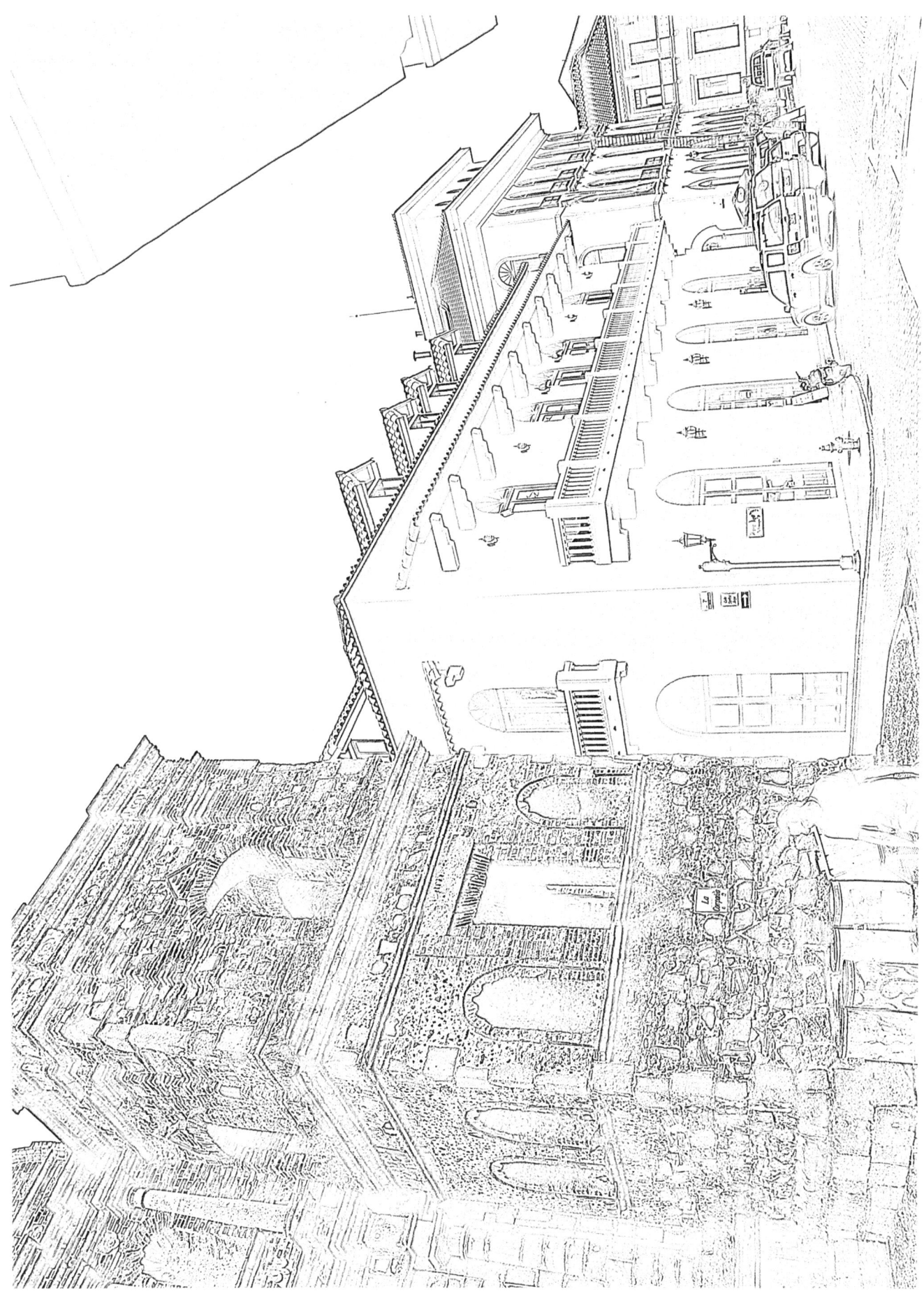

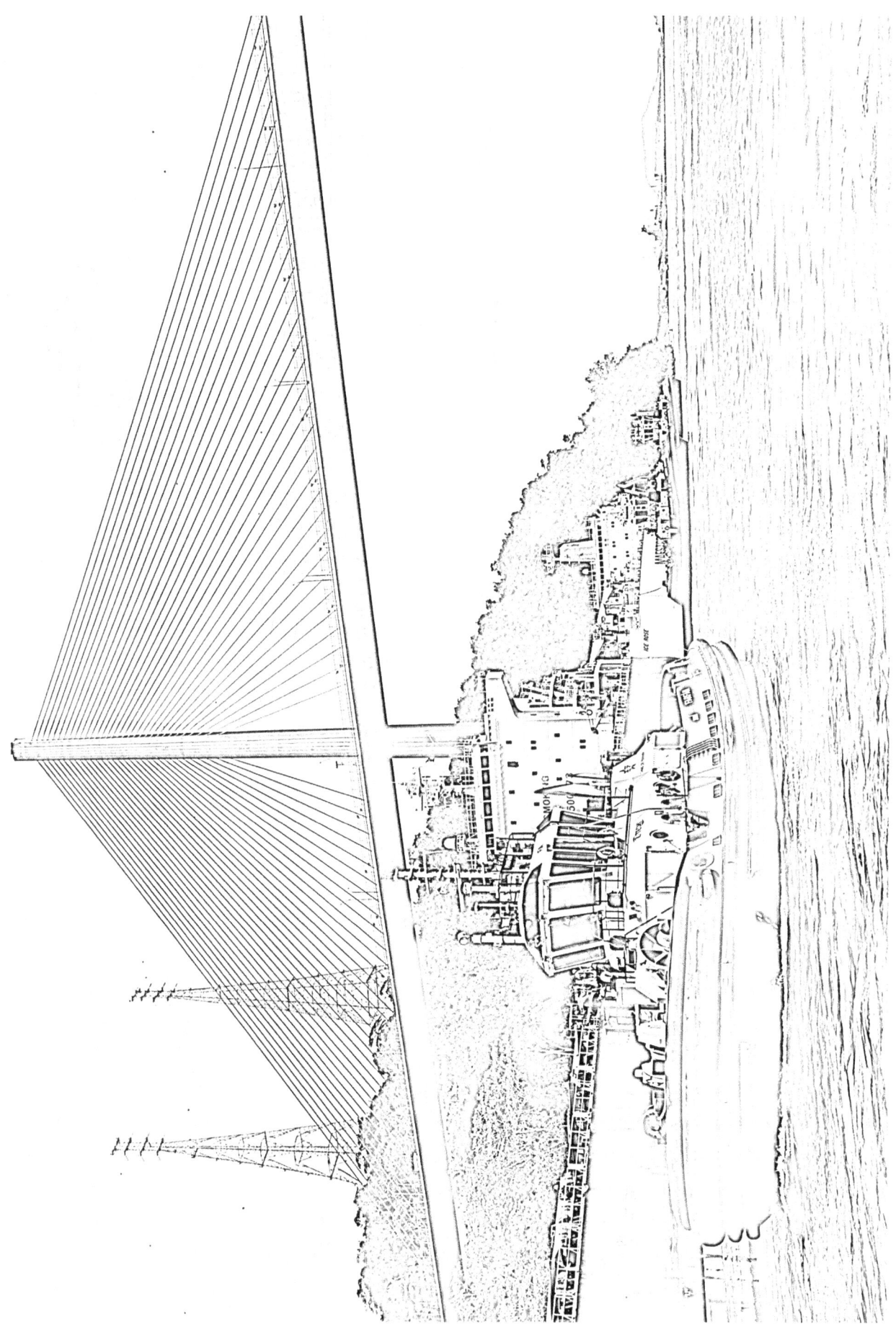

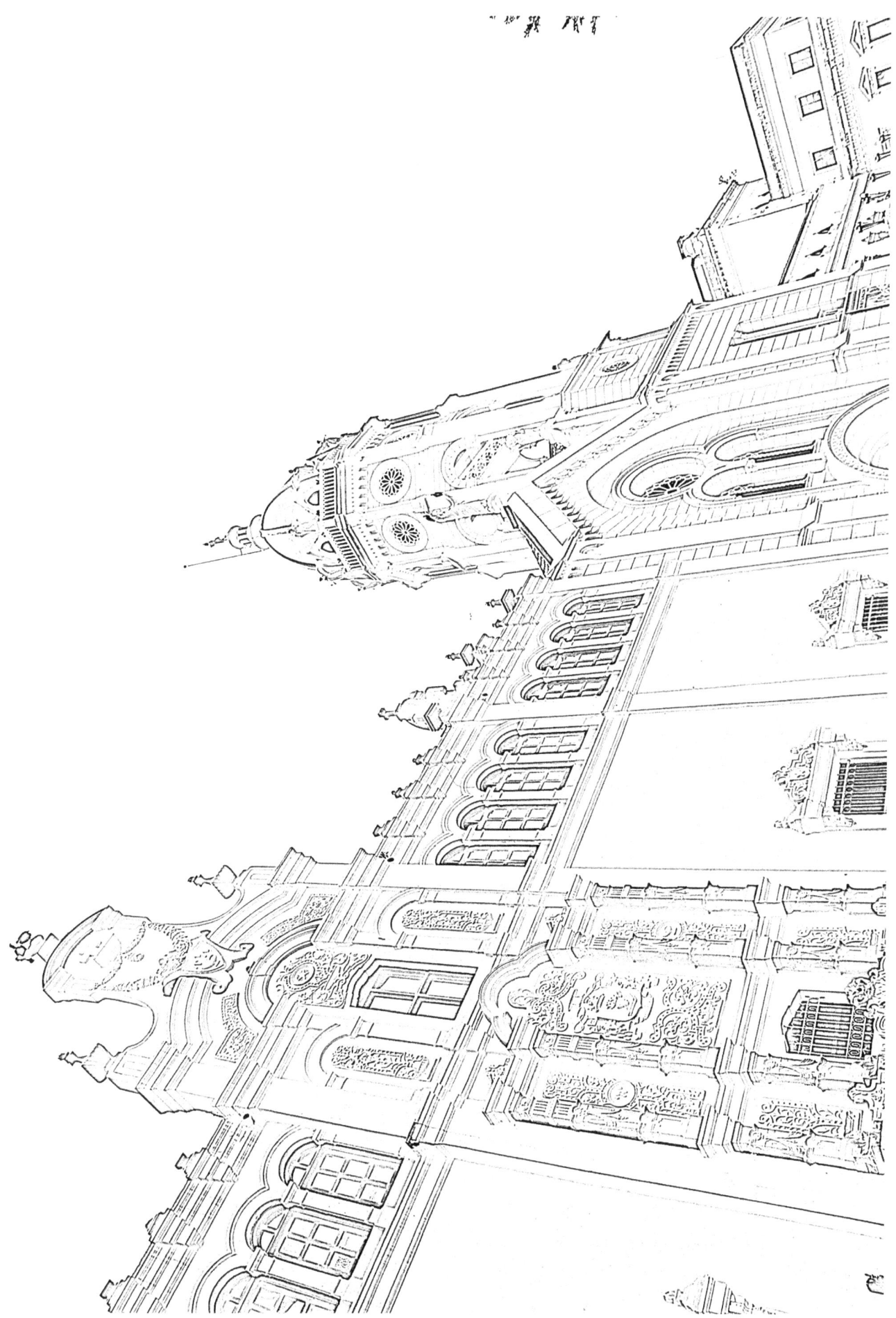

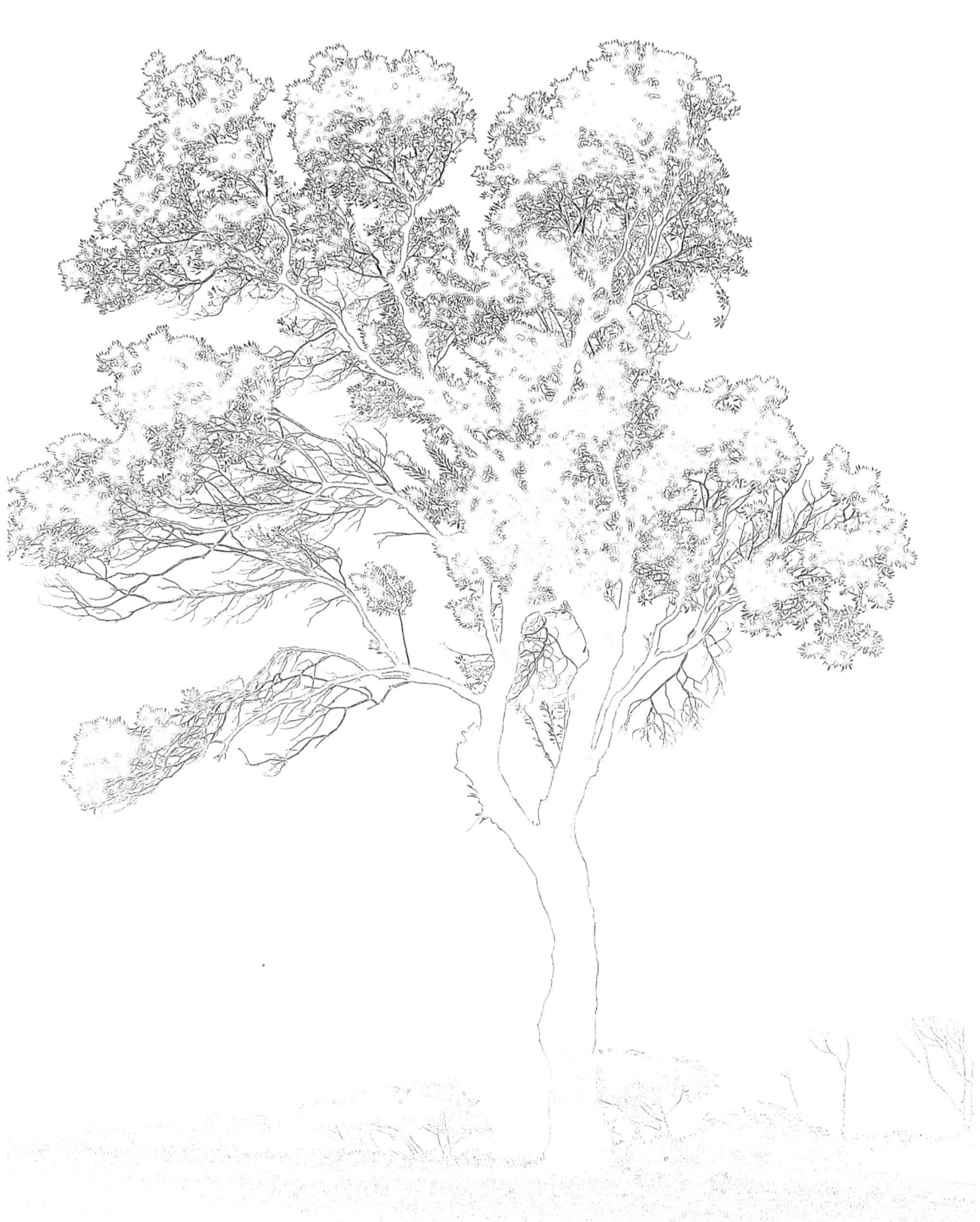

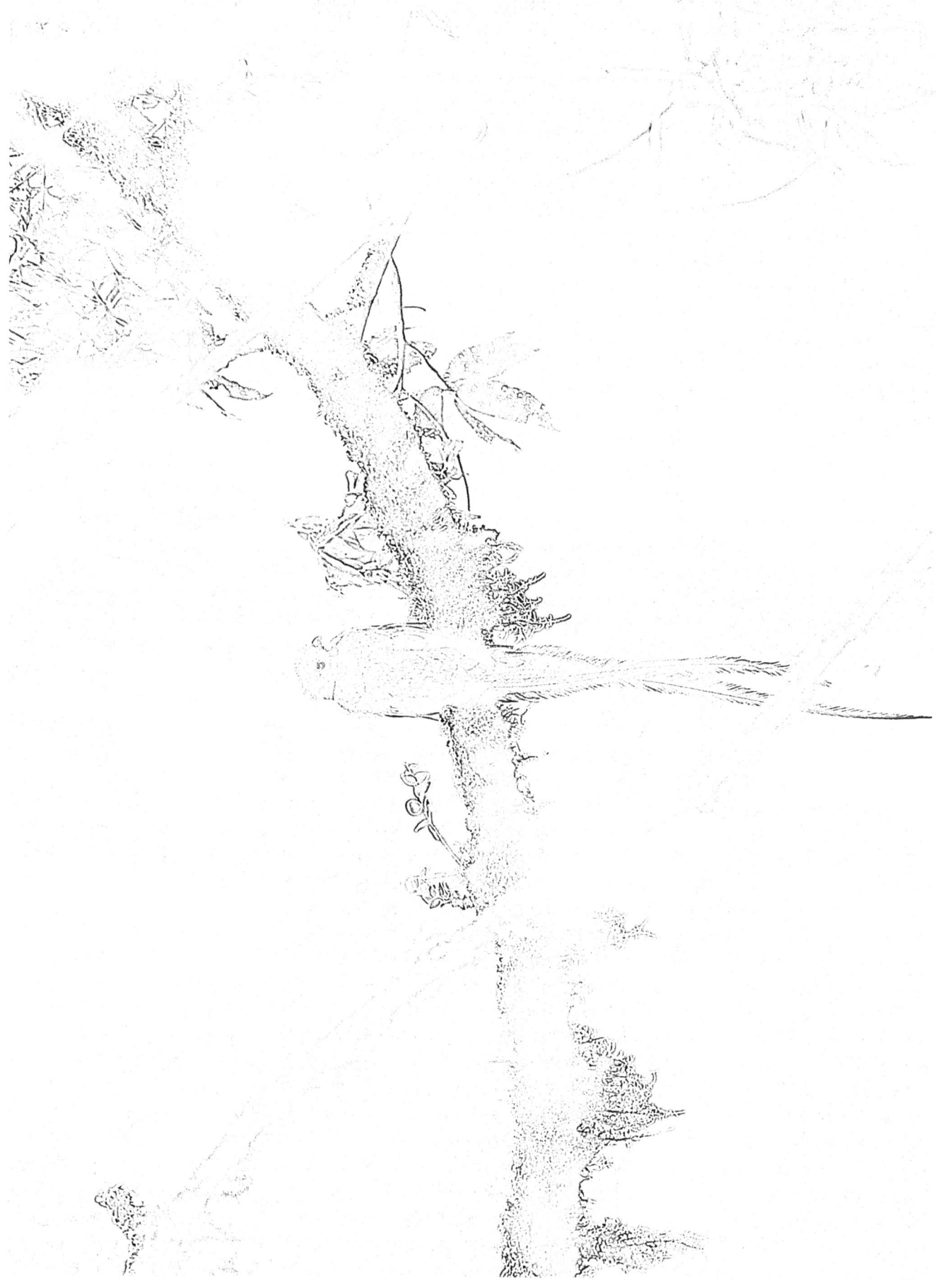

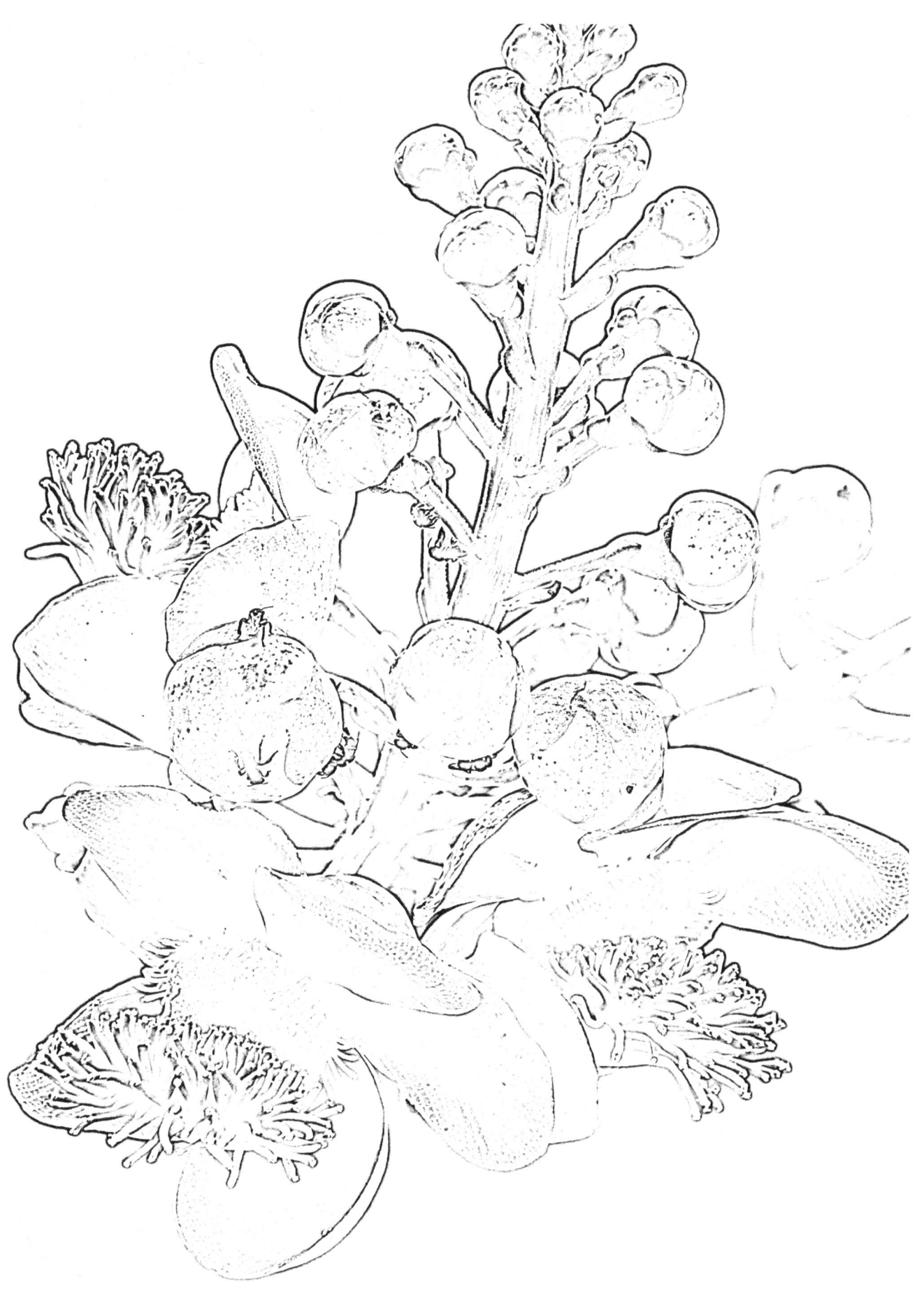

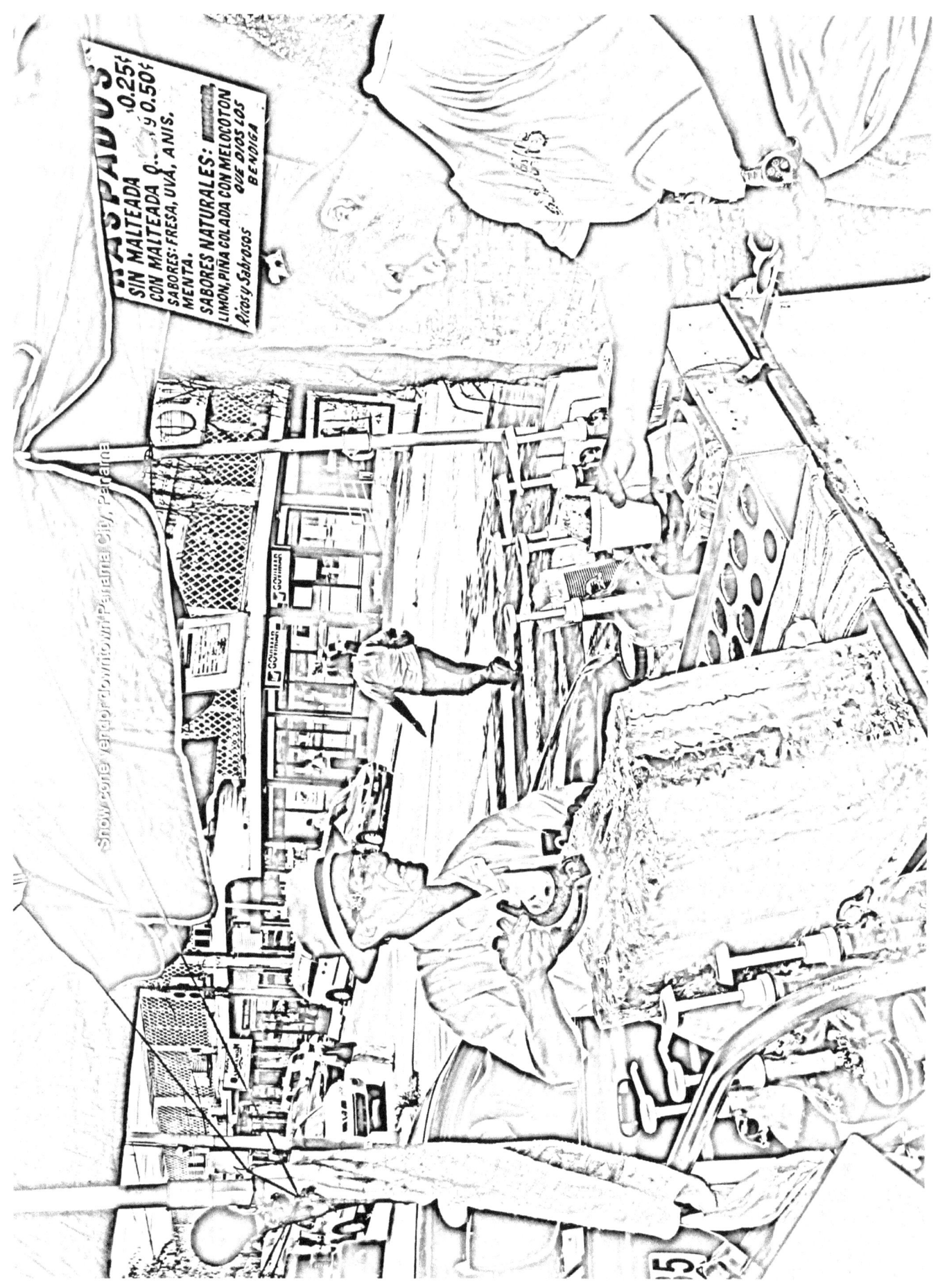

Snow cone vendor downtown Panama City, Panama

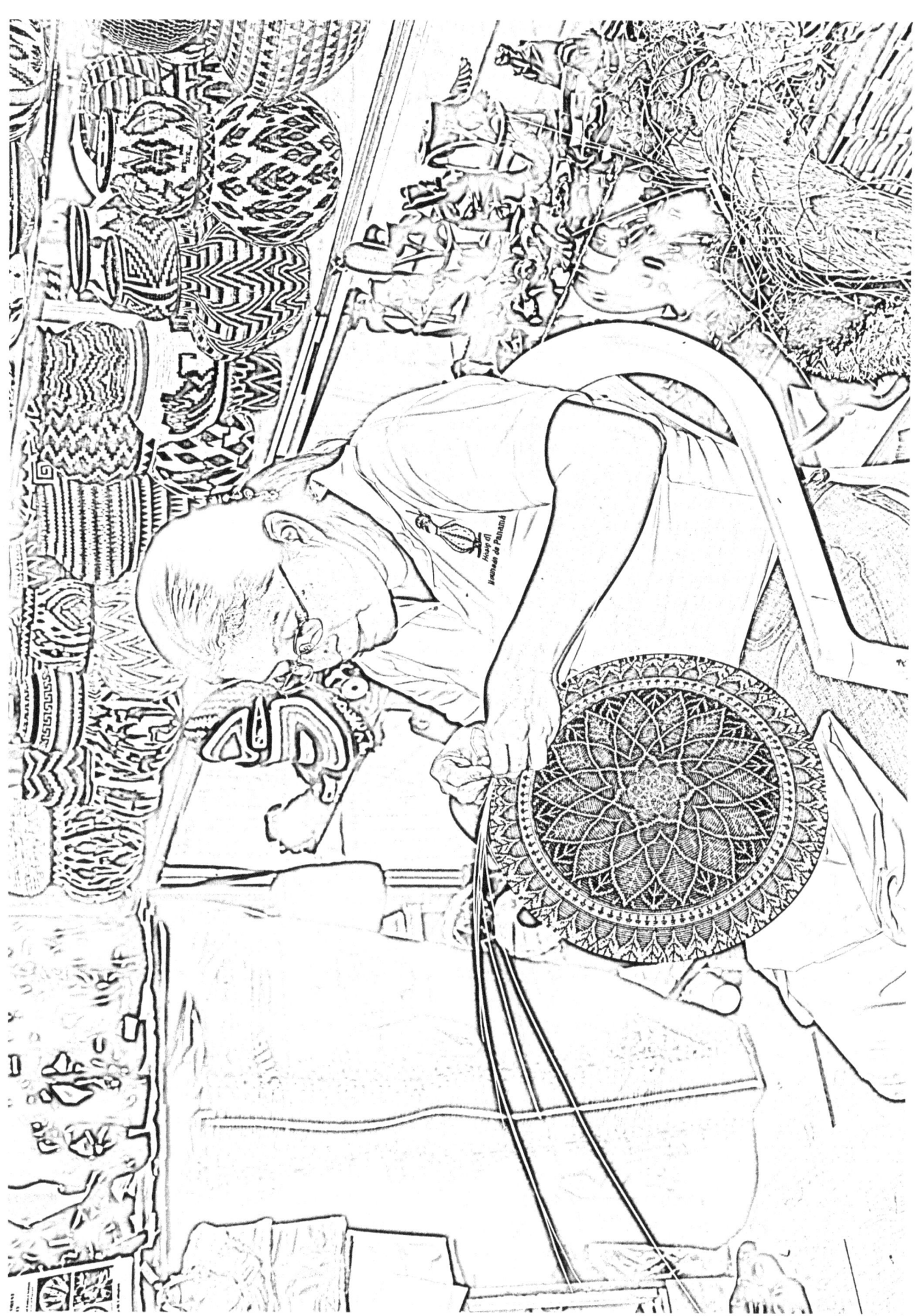

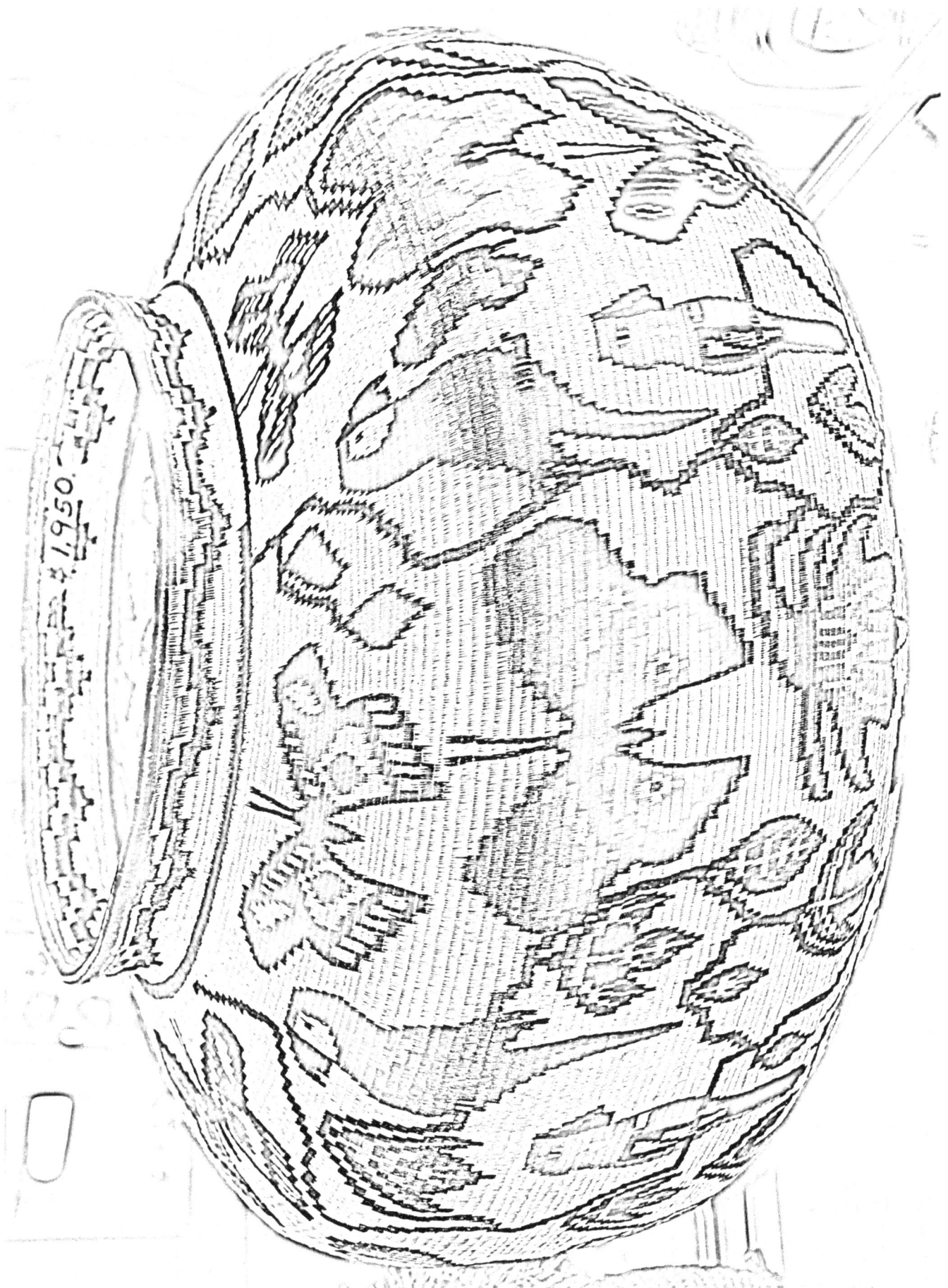

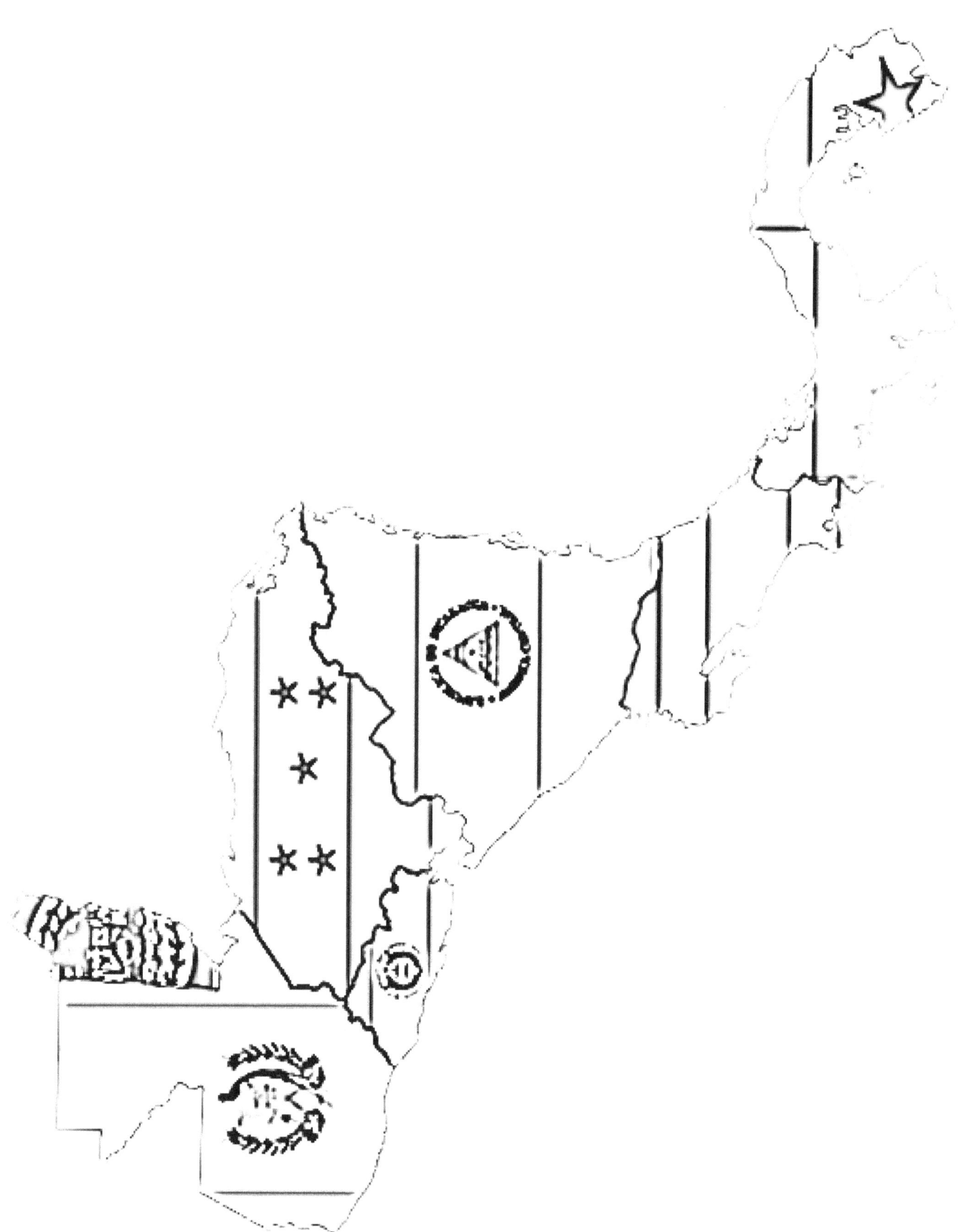

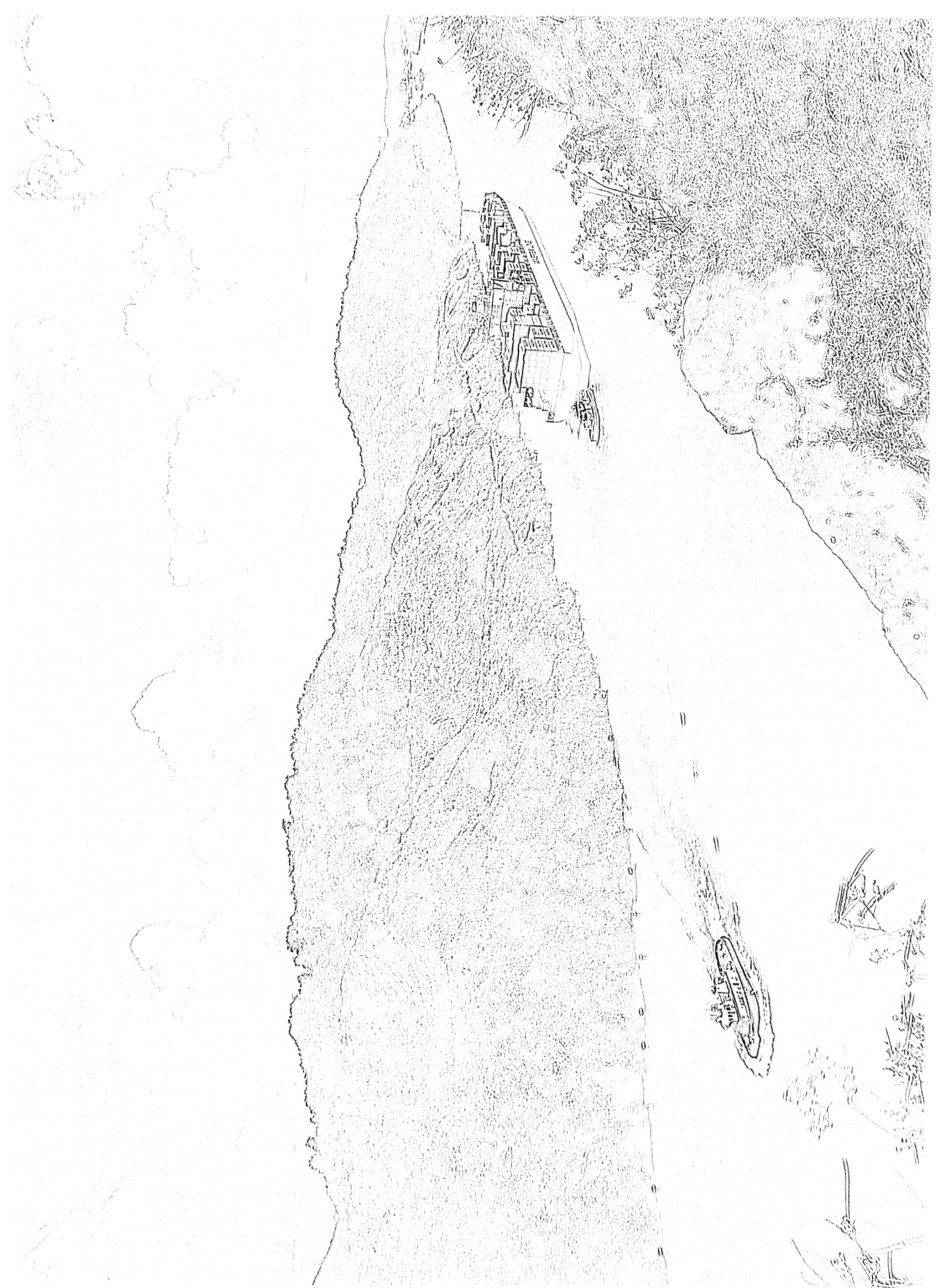

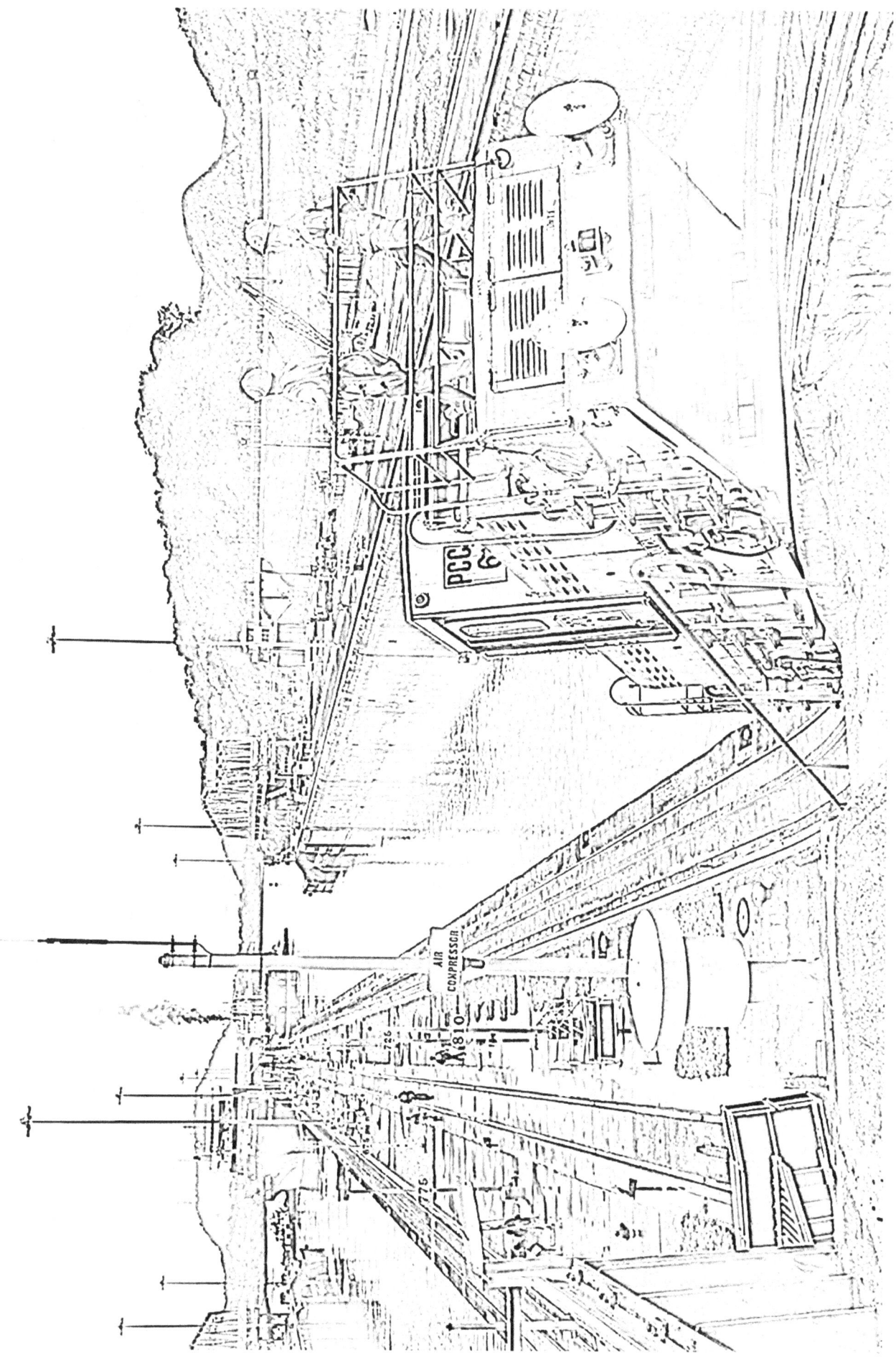

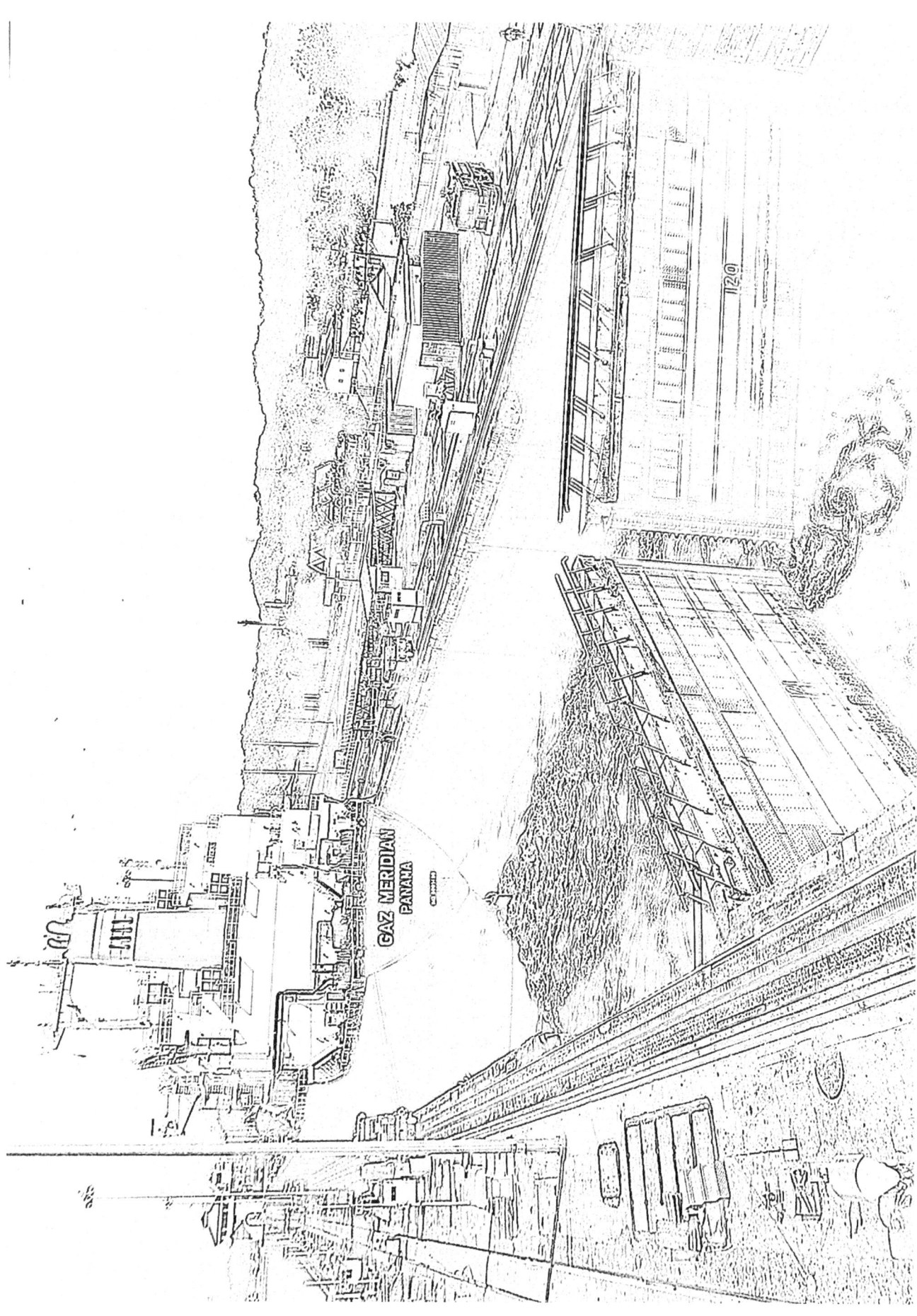

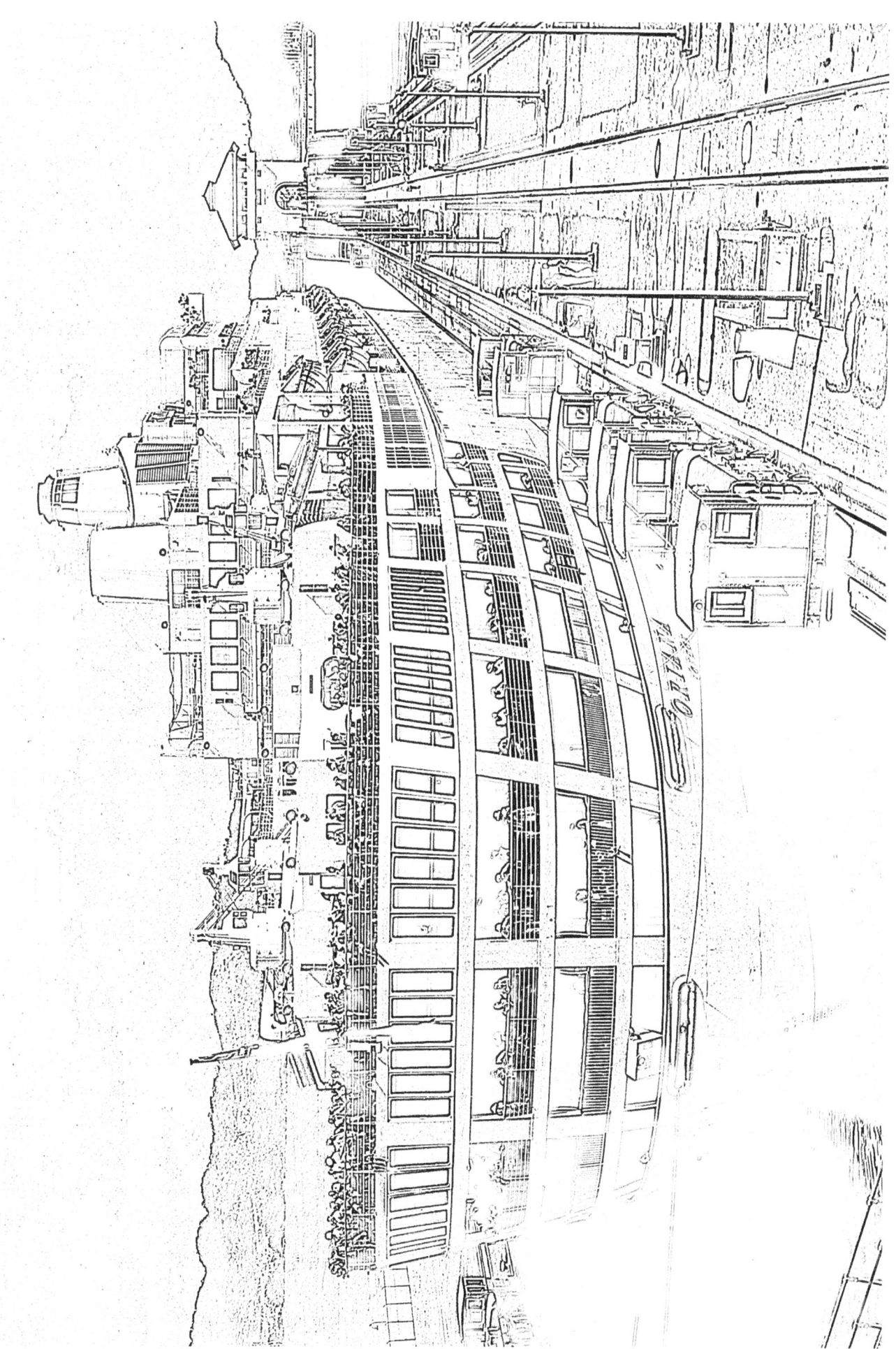

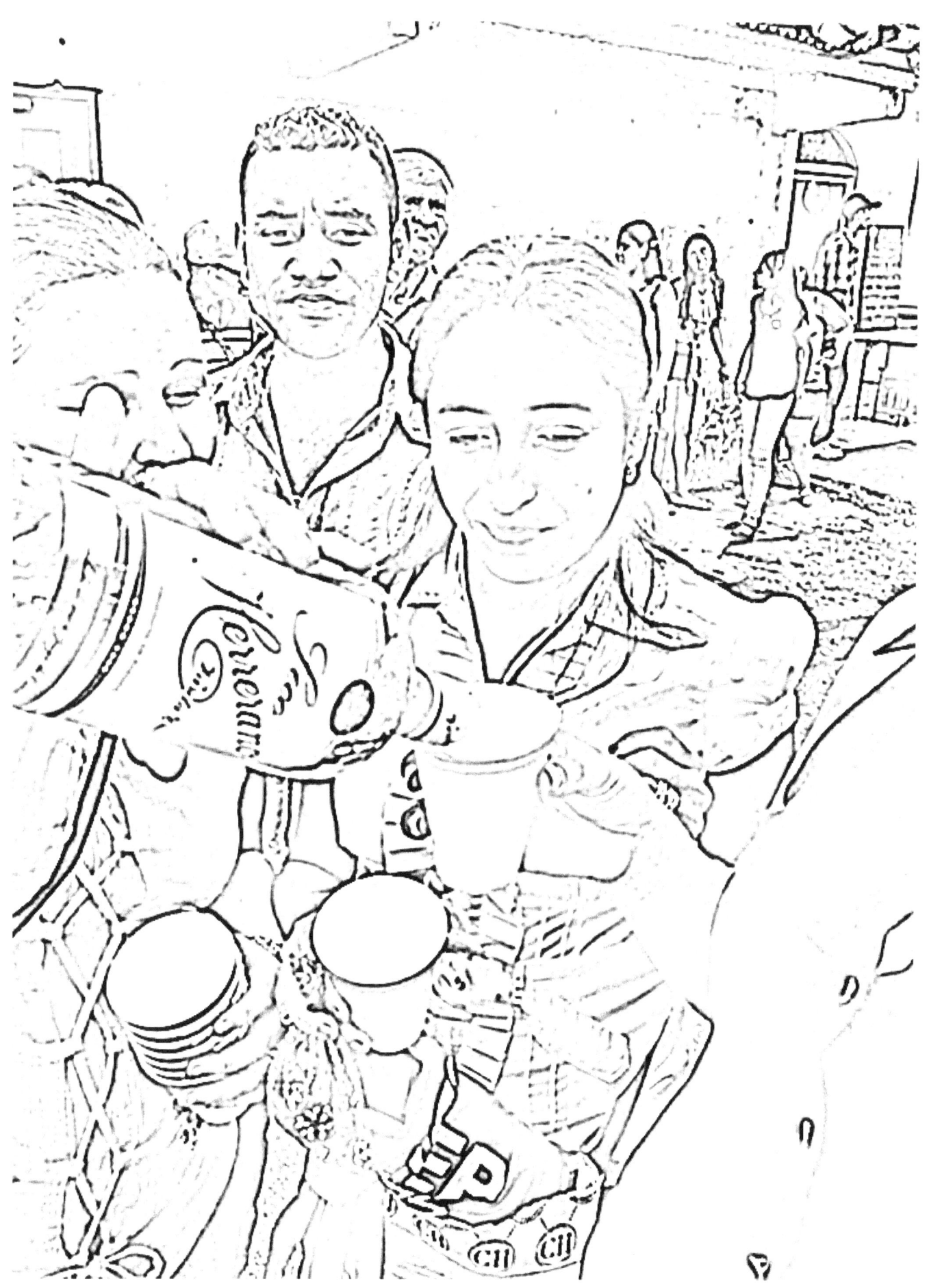

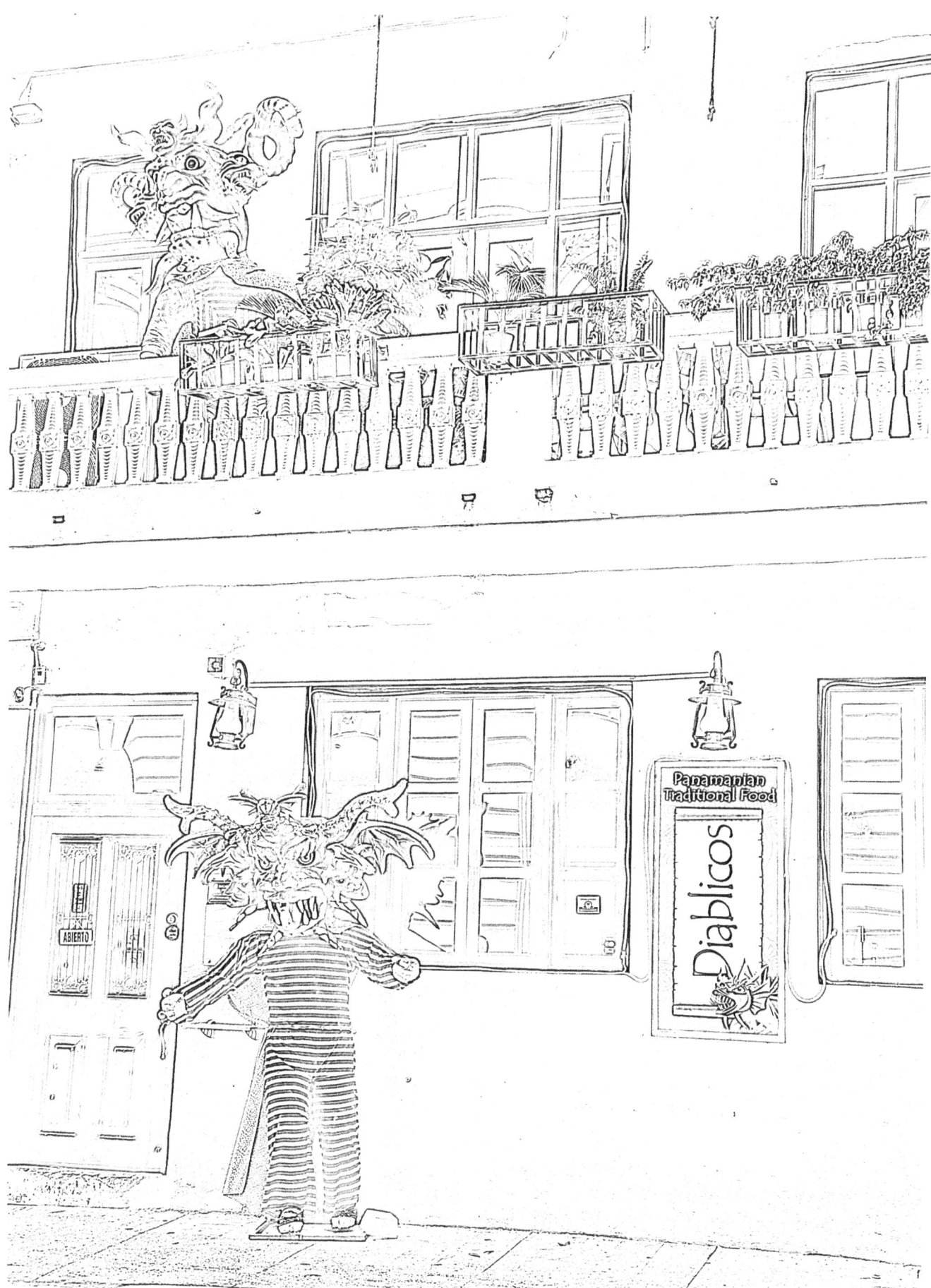

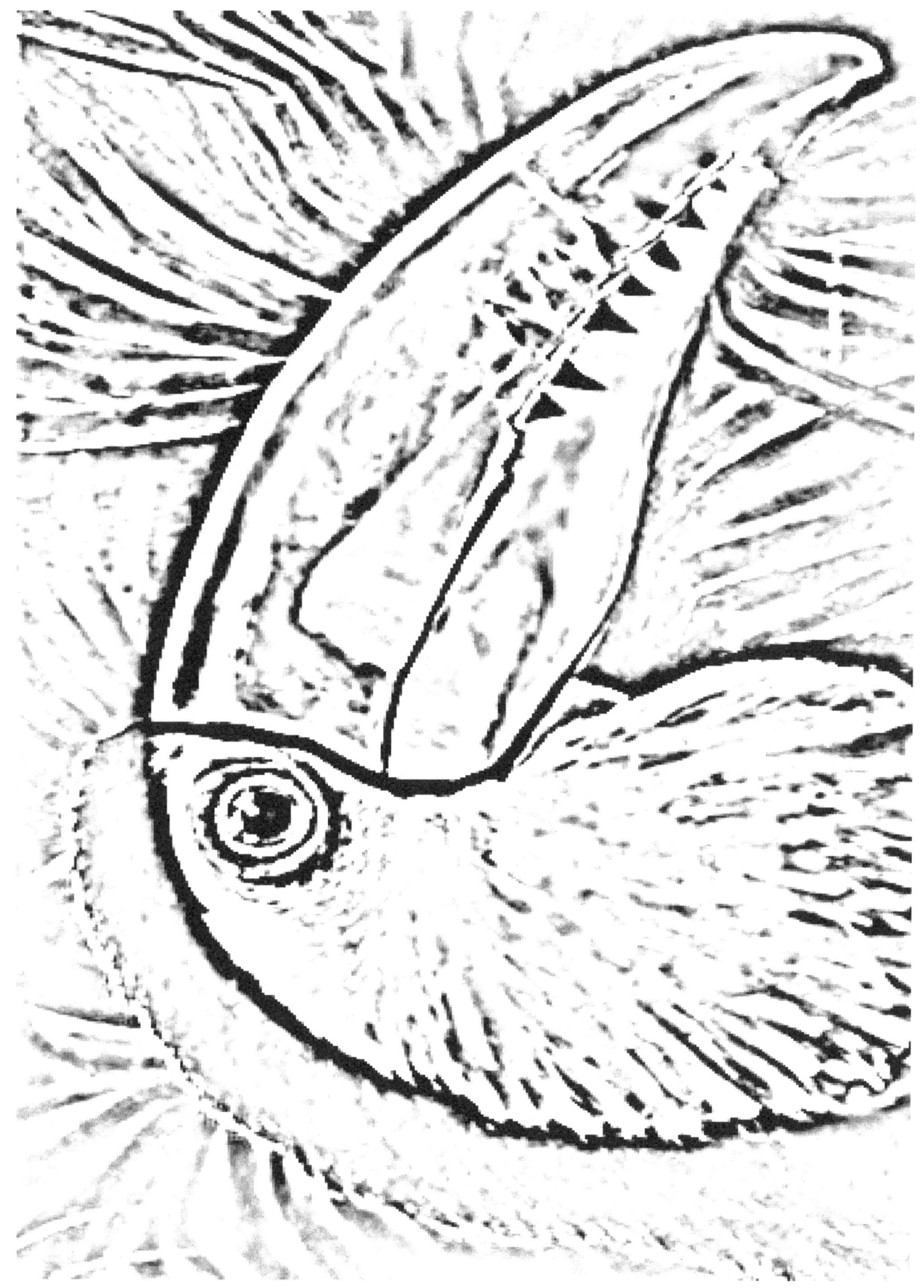

www.ingramcontent.com/pod-product-compliance
Lightning Source LLC
Chambersburg PA
CBHW080827180526
45168CB00006B/2599